JESSE JOHN TOFAH

The Feast Of Weeks

Unveiling the mystery
of the last days

THE FEAST OF WEEKS

Jesse John Tofah

ISBN: 978-9988-3-1579-5

For further information or permission address:

Jesse John Tofah

Mob: +233 50 137 5188

Email: jessetofah@gmail.com

All Scripture quotations are from the King James Version of the Bible, except otherwise stated.

Published and Printed in Ghana

Litemedya@gmail.com

+233 543 989 662

The Feast Of Weeks

Unveiling the mystery
of the last days

JESSE JOHN TOFAH

Dedication

To the body of Christ who is the Church of the living
God; the pillar and ground of the truth

Acknowledgemnt

I stand in awe of God's acts in my life; I owe everything to Him. I would like to immensely thank God for giving me a second chance to putting this book together. I say this because, I almost left writing the book in the middle of the journey. I thank God for upholding me to get through with this book. I am most grateful to my Saviour and LORD Jesus Christ for saving me from sin and death and for giving me this ministry and also for confirming the visions shown me. Then again, I can't thank the Holy Spirit enough for the things He taught and revealed to me in the course of putting this book together. Most of the things in this book, I was taught firsthand by the Holy Spirit; I'd never seen them anywhere or been taught in that fashion. I can't thank God enough. Again I owe it all to Him!

On the other hand, several people have contributed in varying capacity to putting this book together. I would like to thank God for bringing these awesome people my way (in no particular order):

- Ms. Akosua Gyamfuah Duah who served as my accountability partner. Your continuous checking on the progress of the book kept me on my toes.

- Ms. Esther Achampong who served as my senior editor. You worked within a very short time to ensure we met deadlines.

- Pastor Maxwell K. Tofah (Grace Baptist Church - Westland) who reviewed the book. You kept challenging me to know the LORD.

- Pastor Theophilus Degollo (Winners' Chapel International or David Oyedepo Ministries International) who reviewed the book. You run a very tight schedule, yet you made time for the book.

- Mrs. Makafui Hukportie (former Children's Department Superintendent – VBC) who reviewed the book. Your submissions were encouraging to note.

- Sandra Arthur-Kennedy (MD); your walk of faith is contagious. This inspired me on every side.

- Mr. Saviour Agobah and Mr. Derrick Asanate both of LiteMedya who worked long hours to produce the final book and cover design.

- Mr. Richmond Appiah-Kubi my Bible Studies teacher at NUBS-KNUST. I still remember those one-on-one all night Bible sessions.

- Apostle Samuel Obese (Samuel Obese Ministries). Your words of wisdom and counsel have helped me in this phase of life.

- Mr. Ernest Afortokey; you challenged me from an early stage to be a man of prayer.

- Mr. Emmanuel Adjei-Kusi (Keak Studio) for photography.

- Everyone who has been part of this journey.

Contents

Introduction

The Last Days are days of mysteries! One of such mysteries is the mystery of the Feast of Weeks. We are still in the Feast of Weeks! The sickle has already been put to the corn. Seven Sabbaths have been numbered already. It is the fiftieth day of the feast, **THE LAST DAY,** and it's not ended yet. If the glory of the latter house shall be greater than the former; then we are in the day of greater glory of the house of our God. It is too late for the devil to stop the feast. I have sworn by Myself says God, the word is gone out of my mouth in righteousness, and shall not return; that unto Me every knee shall bow, every tongue shall swear (Isa 45:23).

Scripture speaking of the tribe of Issachar says; they were men that had understanding of the times, to know what the children of God ought to do and so were always in command and in the lead (I Chronicles 12:32 paraphrased). Knowledge and wisdom (knowing what to do and doing it) of the times is key in accomplishing all that God has spoken (Isa 33:6 paraphrased), because He (God) has put in His power these times and seasons and those that belong to us are revealed (Acts 1:7; Deut 29:29)

Therefore it is imperative to know and understand that we are **STILL** in the Feast of Weeks and more importantly the fiftieth day of the feast- the climax. And this last day of the feast is the day of the great ingathering as prophesied by both the Prophet Isaiah and Micah:

> *And it shall come to pass in the LAST DAYS, that the mountain of the Lord's house shall be established in the top of the mountains, and shall be exalted above the hills; and ALL NATIONS SHALL FLOW UNTO IT.*

> *And many people shall go and say, Come ye, and let us go up to the mountain of the Lord, to the house of the God of Jacob; and he will teach us of His ways, and we will walk in His paths: for out*

of Zion shall go forth the law, and the word of the Lord from Jerusalem.

Isa 2:2-3

But in the LAST DAYS it shall come to pass, that the mountain of the house of the Lord shall be established in the top of the mountains, and it shall be exalted above the hills; and PEOPLE SHALL FLOW UNTO IT.

AND MANY NATIONS SHALL COME, and say, Come, and let us go up to the mountain of the Lord, and to the house of the God of Jacob; and he will teach us of his ways, and we will walk in his paths: for the law shall go forth of Zion, and the word of the Lord from Jerusalem.

Mic 4:1-2

And we see Jesus Christ corroborate this prophecy in John's gospel chapter twelve verse thirty two:

And I, if I be lifted up from the earth, WILL DRAW ALL MEN UNTO ME.

John 12:32

Has Jesus Christ been lifted up from the earth? Which is to say, has Jesus Christ resurrected from the dead?

The answer is a big YES!

> *For I delivered unto you first of all that which I also received, how that Christ died for our sins according to the scriptures;*
>
> *And that he was buried, and that HE ROSE AGAIN THE THIRD DAY according to the scriptures:*
>
> *1 Cor 15:3-4*

Then John 12:32 is fully operational in our days!

Reading through these scriptures above together with Jesus' words sends the feeling of a huge task and the big question of "Can these things be, seeing all the woes and growing evil and unbelief in God in this generation?" Can I tell you this, you are not the only person who has imagined the magnitude of the work involved and the chances of a blatant failure to achieve the said target. But let it be known that, God is not asking us to do it because we can, rather, because He wants to work through us and this is sure; **"Let God be true and every man a liar**! And let me remind you also, that the popular statement of "with God all things are possible…" as quoted by Jesus Christ was in response to the disciples' question of "who then can be saved?" If Jesus the Christ said it, then He must have figured out how to accomplish this great feat. **Our duty will be to believe His word by following through to the end on how He (God) intends to get this done and by which arsenals.**

This book, by the inspiration of the Holy Ghost who is the owner and author of these words, seeks to remind and make aware that we are still in the Feast of Weeks; more importantly, the last day of that great feast. And like the climax of every great story is usually a happy ending of great things because every vision speaks loudest at the end (Habakkuk 2:3) – much more is this! It is no coincidence that the Church of Jesus Christ has become the center of attention in our days. As such, the devil has employed all means available including human agents to bash the church at the slightest opportunity, targeted at frustrating God's agenda of massive and unprecedented gatherings – **ALL men must come up to the mountain of the house of the LORD.** Can I tell you this, don't fight them with carnal weapons of debates and arguments on whatever platform, rather choose to use what God has provided for this specific task to be achieved which we shall consider in detail! In addition, this book seeks to open us on the Person or Chairman of the feast.

Hallelujah... Jesus is LORD!!

Chapter

one

The Holy Convocations

Speak unto the children of Israel, and say unto them, concerning the feasts of the Lord, which ye shall proclaim to be holy convocations, even these are my feasts.

Leviticus 23:2

Adam had fallen short of the glory of God and the nature of the god-man he was. He was reduced to mortality by sin, out of whom came the host of mankind. The host of creation which was once given to be under his dominion no longer recognized this god-man - Adam. Creation was in chaos and the sins of men multiplied on the earth as men multiplied (Genesis 6:1,5).

God repented of creating mankind (Genesis 6:6) and sent a mighty destruction by flood upon the earth which wiped out everything that had breath upon the surface of the earth saving only a man called Noah and his family and every other living creature upon the earth; the male and the female to keep seed on the earth (Gen 6:17-19).

It was the time after the great destruction of the earth by God. Noah and his family began to repopulate the earth. Through the lineage of Shem, son of Noah, God chose a man by name Abram (Genesis 11:10,26). God called Abram out of a Gentile nation and established His covenant with him (Genesis 12:1-2, 17:4-7). Now God would reveal to Abraham what should happen to his generation after him: "of certainty, your generation after you shall be strangers in a foreign land and there they shall be servants and afflicted for four hundred years. However, in the fullness of time, I will judge those that afflicted them and liberate them from their oppressors. They shall come out of bondage with great possessions and I shall cause them to inherit the land I promised you" (Gen 15:12-14).

In the process of time, all was fulfilled according as the LORD revealed unto Abraham. The descendants of Abraham, Israel, cried because of their bondage in Egypt and God heard them according as he spoke unto Abraham their father. God appeared to Moses, the son of Amran of the tribe of Levi, the son of Jacob, the son of Isaac, the son of Abraham. Moses was commissioned by God to bring Israel out of Egypt (Exodus 3:7-10)

> ***And afterward Moses and Aaron went in, and told Pharaoh, Thus saith the Lord God of Israel, Let my people go, that they may hold a feast unto me in the wilderness***
>
> ***Exodus 5:1***

It is interesting what scripture tells as the motivation of Israel's redemption from Egypt – "***...that they may hold a feast unto me in the wilderness".*** The Holy Convocations or the feasts of the LORD are God's institution to the children of Israel throughout all their generations. Amazingly, God gave these feasts to Israel just when Israel left bondage into liberty. This is an allusion to these convocations as a pattern for God's redemptive agenda. These included:

i.   the Sabbath of rest *(Leviticus 23:3)*
ii. the Lord's Passover *(Leviticus 23:5)*
iii. the feast of unleavened bread *(Leviticus 23:6)*

iv. the feast of weeks *(Leviticus 23:15,16,21)*
v.   the blowing of trumpets *(Leviticus 23:24)*
vi. the day of atonement *(Leviticus 23:27)*
vii. the feast of tabernacles *(Leviticus 23:34)*

Now these marked specific calendar events in the history of the nation Israel. But God in His infinite wisdom was more than just marking calendar events in the nation of Israel, rather these patterned God's calendar for the entire human race, Israel being the seed or the means. A closer look at these Holy Convocations reveal an interesting pattern concerning God's agenda to redeem the whole of mankind. It is worth mentioning that some of these have been fulfilled already; the Lord's Passover (Leviticus 23:5) and the feast of unleavened bread (Leviticus 23:6). We are now in the Feast of Weeks and must add, the latter part of it!

Now I will need you to pay close attention to how God reveals His plan in Moses to Israel – a type of the Church.

Fear and dread shall fall upon them; by the greatness of thine arm they shall be as still as a *stone; **till thy people pass over, O Lord, till the people pass over, which thou hast purchased***

***Thou shalt bring them in, and plant them in the mountain of Thine inheritance, in the place**, O Lord, which Thou hast made for Thee to dwell in, in the Sanctuary, O Lord, which Thy hands have established.*

The Lord shall reign for ever and ever

Exodus 15:16-18

In verse sixteen through to eighteen of Exodus chapter fifteen, the prophet Moses speaks of the Passover and "the bring in and plant in" and immediately in the next verse, he prophesies of the mountain of God's inheritance - the Church. Thus the Passover and "the bring in and plant in" is the outdooring of the Church in what would be the Feast of Weeks according to God's redemptive calendar for the entire human race. This clearly, again, is an indication of the Holy Convocation as a pattern for God's great redemption. In subsequent chapters when we shall look at the subject matter – "The Feast of Weeks" in detail, we shall examine the place the LORD has chosen to dwell which is one crucial aspect in the fulfilment of the prophecy foretold.

Follow me as we examine these Holy Convocations in brief so as to help us appreciate the Feast of Weeks.

The Sabbath Of Rest

> *Six days shall work be done: but the seventh day is the Sabbath of rest, an holy convocation; ye shall do no work therein: it is the Sabbath of the Lord in all your dwellings.*
>
> *Leviticus 23:3*

The Sabbath of rest is celebrated to mark the day God rested from His work when He created the heaven and the earth and ordered all that is therein. Thus six days God worked and on the seventh day God rested from all His labour (Exodus 20:10-11). In honouring this day, God commands that no work be done by any man or animal in Israel – it is a most holy day in all their generations (Exodus 31:13-16). In the book of Deuteronomy chapter five verse fourteen and fifteen, scripture reveals the purpose of the Sabbath of rest – *"that you and all of Israel may rest"*.

> *But the seventh day is the Sabbath of the Lord thy God: in it thou shalt not do any work, thou, nor thy son, nor thy daughter, nor thy manservant, nor thy maidservant, nor thine*

ox, nor thine ass, nor any of thy cattle, nor thy stranger that is within thy gates; that thy manservant and thy maidservant may rest as well as thou.

And remember that thou was a servant in the land of Egypt, and that the Lord thy God brought thee out thence through a mighty hand and by a stretched out arm: therefore the Lord thy God commanded thee to keep the Sabbath day.

Deuteronomy 5:14 - 15

At the end of the *"sixth"* is the end of all forms of oppressions, servitude, slavery and bondage. The *"seventh"* ushers in rest – *"there shall be no work"* - signifying redemption, freedom and liberty. It is no surprise that Jesus Christ, the Saviour of the whole world, comes in at the beginning of the **"seventh sevens"** and leaves just before the end of the *"seventh sevens"* as we shall consider in detail in chapter 2. By the Sabbath of rest, God outlined to Israel, the seed, to the end, His day of rest!   Rest from oppression, servitude, slavery and bondage!!

Now, the underlining concept of servitude is obedience to whosoever is lord over you! The Apostle Paul puts it this way; "do you not know that whosoever you yield yourselves to obey, his servants you are?" (Rom 6:16). In other words, God would mean to the children of Israel – you are **masters** in a free land now not as you were servants put under taskmasters in the land of Egypt to obey them. You are of yourselves in dominion as I gave to Adam at creation when he (Adam) was in his rest (the Garden of Eden)! In a typical scenario of servitude, those held, had no control of their own and were put under the control of their masters because it is required of servants to obey their masters (Col 3:22). Thus the statement **"...*that thou was a servant in the land of Egypt*"** suggests that the present circumstance is not as the former and essentially the opposite of the same. Therefore it was necessary to remind Israel and by extension the Church of Jesus Christ by the Sabbath of rest that they were masters of their own "creation" no longer under servitude to obey Egypt, a type of the body of sin. More importantly, they are put to assume responsibility in fulfillment of God's will here on earth. A constant reminder of the liberty to now obey God is important to rid their minds of the acquired culture and behaviours of servitude and to create the awareness of their new found freedom to live as such. I can imagine the damage of what four hundred and thirty years of servitude, oppression, affliction and worst of it, the continuous exposure to the worship of idols which was the order of the day in Egypt, could have done to their minds and self-image. They could not be in charge to call the shot, decide the course of action as best fit and tops serve God as God would have them. But now, we are made free from sin and have become servants to God (Rom 6:22). Through this avenue, Israel would remind themselves of what rest God purchased for them by His mighty hand and outstretched arm. I perceive they would say to themselves – I am free, I am free, I am free; no longer a servant to Egypt!

But is that all there is to the Sabbath of Rest? In the book of Hebrews, chapters three and four, we are told that they did not actualize this rest God promised them (Hebrews 3:9-11, 18). Rather, in the land of freedom, they entangled themselves again with the body of sin, living after the manner of Egypt and in their hearts they returned to Egypt (Acts 7:39). Therefore did they not enter into the rest; *the rest of the Garden of Eden*, the rest from sin and its woes, the rest from bondage and servitude, the rest of the promised land, the rest of God's blessings as listed in *Deuteronomy 28:1-14*. On several occasions, by reason of their disobedience, they were taken back into captivity. On that wise, scripture speaks of the promise of another rest reserved for those who have believed (Hebrews 4:1,3,9) – that is our hope! The caution here is this, we who have believed, **labour** to enter into this rest so we are not taken unaware by the same trap of unbelief. Thus the Church of the last days must pay close attention, for these things are written afore for our learning that we through patience and comfort may have hope – the hope of God's rest reserved for the redeemed.

The Sabbath of rest therefore on the calendar event marks the beginning and end of God's great redemptive plan – *looking at the calendar as cyclical, starting with the Sabbath of rest, because God had rested from His work, and ending with same, because we the redeemed are awaiting our rest.* When the feast of Tabernacles (see page 31) is fulfilled when we shall dwell (tabernacle) with the LORD together in heaven, all who have believed Jesus Christ as Saviour shall enter into this Sabbath of rest forever and shall cease from our work (Hebrews 4:10).

The Lord's Passover

This month shall be unto you the beginning of months: it shall be the first month of the year to you.

And thus shall ye eat it; with your loins girded, your shoes on your feet, and your staff in your hand; and ye shall eat it in haste: **it is the Lord's Passover.**

For I will pass through the land of Egypt this night, and will smite all the firstborn in the land of Egypt, both man and beast; and against all the gods of Egypt I will execute judgment: I am the Lord.

And the blood shall be to you for a token upon the houses where ye are: and **when I see the blood, I will pass over** *you,* **and the plague shall not be upon you to destroy you,** *when I smite the land of Egypt.*

And this day shall be unto you for a memorial; and ye shall keep it a feast to the Lord

throughout your generations; ye shall keep it a feast by an ordinance forever.

And it came to pass at the end of the four hundred and thirty years, even the selfsame day it came to pass, that all the hosts of the Lord went out from the land of Egypt.

It is a night to be much observed unto the Lord for bringing them out from the land of Egypt: this is that night of the Lord to be observed of all the children of Israel in their generations.

Exodus 12:2, 11-14, 41-42

Next on the calendar events of God's great redemptive plan is the Feast of the Lord's Passover – strategic in positioning. Reasonably so, the rest of the Sabbath has been spoken of; it is that time to roll out the accomplishment of same following through with the Feast of the Lord's Passover. By this time, Israel had been in captivity in Egypt for four hundred and thirty years. This indeed had been a long time! But finally, their redemption was nearer than they first imagined. It was a night to be much remembered.

The central theme of the Feast of Passover was to bring judgment by the blood upon Egypt and their gods that had held Israel bound these four hundred and thirty years and consequently cause their freedom. Remember that this was God's covenant with Abraham in Genesis 15:12-14. For those that oppressed them all these years, the LORD judged and not only that, He made an utter end of them. This destruction crippled the entire Egypt – killed every firstborn both man and beast taking away their source of strength, power and posterity; for that's what the firstborn represented (Gen 49:3). That never again would they dare hold the children of God in captivity. Therefore it is written; sin (a type of Egypt) shall not have dominion over you (Rom 6:14)! By the blood of the covenant, even the blood of the Lamb of God – Jesus the Christ, the Passover was enforced and Israel left Egypt finally after such a long time! The blood is the stronghold of the covenant!! We are told in the book of *Numbers 33:3 "And they departed from Rameses in the first month, on the fifteenth day of the first month; on the morrow after the Passover the children of Israel went out with an high hand in the sight of all the Egyptians.*

How does this apply to the Church? In the book of I Corinthians 5:7, scripture speaking says: that Christ has been made to us our Passover. Meaning, that by the blood of Jesus Christ through his crucifixion on the cross, the hold of sin which enslaved the host of mankind has been destroyed and we who were held by it are entered into liberty like Israel in Egypt. And by extension, we have escaped that great destruction coming. To this end, God has been sending the warning message of that sore destruction coming! There is a grave destruction coming!! It coming upon **"sin"** and all its players like it did upon Egypt. The only escape is by the blood of Jesus Christ, our Passover. That was the only way Israel though in Egypt escaped that great destruction that came upon Egypt. So the only way out is by believing the LORD Jesus Christ that He died to shed His blood for the remission of your sins and on the third day rose up from the grave for your justification (Acts 16:31, Rom 4:24-25, I Cor 15:4, II Cor 4:14). Then;

> ***"...the plague shall not be upon you to destroy you"***
>
> ***Exodus 12:13***

That is to say, until the blood of the Lamb of God, Jesus Christ, is upon you by faith in the finished work of Jesus Christ on the cross, you are not a candidate for exemption from the great destruction coming!

Fear and dread shall fall upon them; by the greatness of thine arm they shall be as still as a stone; **till thy people pass over, O Lord, till the people pass over, which thou hast purchased.**

Thou shalt bring them in, and plant them in the mountain of thine inheritance, in the place, O Lord, which thou hast made for thee to dwell in, in the Sanctuary, O Lord, which thy hands have established.

Exodus 15:16-17

Now to the big one; the ultimate of the Passover revealed in scripture in the book of Exodus chapter fifteen verse sixteen to seventeen is to bring in and plant the purchased of God in the mountain of God, clearly stated here as the *"Sanctuary"*. This brings us again to the prophecy foretold that in the last days the mountain of the house of the LORD shall be established upon the top of the mountains. Meaning, the Church of Jesus Christ shall be prominent in all areas of human endeavour both spiritual and physical dimensions. It is no surprise that since Israel left Egypt, it has become the center of attention throughout history and even much more is the emergence of the Church in Jerusalem since the time of Pentecost.

The Church of Jesus Christ has become the centre of attention gaining growing global influence. In those early days, they said to Peter and the other apostles that they have filled the whole of Jerusalem with their doctrine – the gospel of Jesus Christ! (Acts 5:28). On another occasion, it was reported that almost the whole city gathered together to hear the word of God (Acts 13:44). In contemporary times, we have mega Churches making global impacts to reckon with. This is why the devil fears the Church! You would agree with me that everywhere the gospel of Jesus Christ and for that matter the Church has held the fort, peace, development, progress among others has been the end result. Hallelujah; glory to God! What an awesome God!!

The Feast of Unleavened Bread

> *And in the first day there shall be an holy convocation, and in the seventh day there shall be an holy convocation to you; no manner of work shall be done in them, save that which every man must eat, that only may be done of you.* **And ye shall observe the feast of unleavened bread; for in this selfsame day have I brought your armies out of the land of Egypt: therefore shall**

> *ye observe this day in your generations by an ordinance forever.*
>
> *Exodus 12:16-17*

Following the Passover night when Israel left Egypt is the Feast of Unleavened Bread. Seven days shall none eat of anything made of leaven or be found with leaven (Deut 16:4). And this is to be observed in all of Israel forever! Why would the LORD command such and of what importance is it? In the book of Deuteronomy 16:3, we are told:

> *Thou shalt eat no leavened bread with it; seven days shalt thou eat unleavened bread therewith, even the bread of affliction; for thou camest forth out of the land of Egypt in haste: that thou mayest remember the day when thou camest forth out of the land of Egypt all the days of thy life.*

According to scripture, Israel was to remember **the day** they came out of Egypt all the days of their life! But more importantly the manner of their sudden release; ...*"for thou camest forth out* of the land of Egypt *in haste: that thou mayest remember the day when thou camest forth..."* Thus God wanting to show unto Israel the manner of their sudden release from bondage and slavery demonstrated it in a quick work! That in the matter of the shortest time possible Israel was freed. "In the selfsame day" from ***Exodus 12:17*** underpins this to mean in literal terms – that within the snap of a finger, I brought you out of Egypt, out of four hundred and thirty years of slavery and bondage! And this is what Moses referred to as "the bring in and plant in" according to Exodus 15:17. In the book of Exodus chapter twelve verses thirty three, scripture speaking says:

> ***And the Egyptians were urgent upon the people, that they might send them out of the land in haste; for they said, we be all dead men.***
>
> ***Exodus 12:33***

That is to say it doesn't take God time to set free the captive. He specializes in suddenly saving the lost – and the times we find ourselves has been wrought the sudden work of salvation for the whole of mankind! We see a vivid demonstration of this at the time of the Unleavened Bread in the New Testament from the Acts of the Apostles chapter twelve verse one through to eleven.

Now about that time Herod the king stretched forth his hands to vex certain of the church.

And he killed James the brother of John with the sword.

*And because he saw it pleased the Jews, **he proceeded further to take Peter also. THEN WERE THE DAYS OF UNLEAVENED BREAD.***

*And when he had apprehended him, **he put him in prison, and delivered him to four quaternions of soldiers to keep him**; intending after Easter to bring him forth to the people.*

Peter therefore was kept in prison: but prayer was made without ceasing of the church unto God for him.

And when Herod would have brought him forth, THE SAME NIGHT Peter was sleeping between two soldiers, bound with two chains: and the keepers before the door kept the prison.

*And, behold, the angel of the Lord came upon him, and a light shined in the prison: and he smote Peter on the side, and raised him up, saying, **Arise up quickly**. And his chains fell off from his hands.*

And the angel said unto him, **Gird thyself, and bind on thy sandals.** *And so he did. And he saith unto him, Cast thy garment about thee, and follow me.*

And he went out, and followed him; **and wist not that it was true which was done by the angel;** *but thought he saw a vision.*

When they were past the first and the second ward, they came unto the iron gate that leadeth unto the city; which opened to them of his own accord: and they went out, and passed on through one street; and forthwith the angel departed from him.

And when Peter was come to himself, he said, **now I know of a surety, that the Lord hath sent his angel, and hath delivered me out of the hand of Herod, and from all the expectation of the people of the Jews**

Now note the use of the words "the same night", "quickly" used to describe Peter's sudden escape from death. So you would recognize that like in the case of Israel, that same night, God wrought a quick work to stop Herod from killing Peter the next morning.

Another example is the Apostle Paul on his way to Damascus to persecute the disciples who believed in Jesus Christ (...*And as he journeyed, he came near Damascus:* **and suddenly** *there shined round about him a light from heaven... Acts 9:3.*) Consequently, Paul was saved and he who once persecuted the believers became one of the chief apostles. This is the LORD's doing – hallelujah! I perceive Israel on their way out of Egypt will begin to ask themselves if it were real like Peter who could not believe the sudden escape and thought he saw a vision. How on earth did Pharaoh allow them to go for free? To prove that God didn't require time to bring salvation to anyone who so desires it.

The story is no different from the present day. Believe it or not, the LORD has done a quick work! Though the work be enormous, yet the LORD has done a quick work and will finish it in righteousness (Rom 9:28).This foretells of the urgency with which the LORD has moved to save in these last days. Remember that we have established that the Holy Convocations which includes the Feast of Unleavened Bread are by God's own design a master pattern for the salvation of mankind, Israel being the seed or means to achieve that. Therefore, let us keep the feast with the unleavened bread of sincerity and truth (I Cor 5:7-8)

The Feast of Weeks

Seven weeks shalt thou number unto thee: **begin to number the seven weeks from such time as thou begin to put the sickle to the corn.**

And thou shalt keep the feast of weeks unto the Lord thy God *with a tribute of a freewill offering of thine hand, which thou shalt give unto the Lord thy God, according as the Lord thy God hath blessed thee:*

And thou shalt rejoice before the Lord thy God, thou, and thy son, and thy daughter, and thy manservant, and thy maidservant, and the Levite that is within thy gates, and the stranger, and the fatherless, and the widow, that are among you, **in the place which the Lord thy God hath chosen to place His name there.**

And thou shalt remember that thou was a bondman in Egypt: *and thou shalt observe and do these statutes.*

Deuteronomy 16:9-12

The Feast of Weeks is the fourth on the list of the seven holy convocations as the LORD gave Israel. It sits at the center and the resultant of which shall be the last three feasts – the Feast of Trumpets, the Feast of Atonement and the Feast of Tabernacles. We are in the Feast of Weeks! These are the days of mammoth ingathering of souls into the kingdom of God. The Feast of Unleavened Bread, that is, the quick work of redemptions, has ushered in the Feast of Weeks culminating in the massive ingathering of the harvest!! Interesting also is that the first three have been fulfilled and the times we find ourselves as by God's pattern is the Feast of Weeks (we shall see the proofs of that in the next chapter). In the meantime let's consider some key aspects of what it is.

God instructs specifically when he had brought Israel out of Egypt, the land of slavery, on how to reap, that is, to gather the harvest when they came into the Promised Land. On the day after the Sabbath, the Priest would present the firsts of the fruits to the LORD waving it as a testimony. This is significant as it sets the tone for numbering seven Sabbaths plus one day making a total of fifty days. (We shall consider the mysteries behind these in the chapter on "The

Mysteries of the Feast of Weeks"). On the fiftieth day of the feast which is also the last day, then shall an offering be made unto the LORD (Leviticus 23:16).

In Exodus chapter three verse ten, God says to Moses:

> *Come now therefore, and I will send thee unto Pharaoh that* **thou mayest bring forth my people the children of Israel out of Egypt**
>
> ***Exodus 3:10***

In this place God introduces His ingathering agenda – to bring the people of Israel out of a foreign land into their own land of freedom. He says to Moses, in plain language, bring my people out of the land of slavery and bondage. Now this is akin to the slavery and bondage sin has placed on mankind since the fall of Adam. Every one served in sin and couldn't be freed no matter what they did. You woke up every day to be greeted with the struggles of sin. The spirit man who is the real being was dead, the soul was corrupted and the body grew weaker and weaker to sin. Imagine a world where there was no window for sin as such the tenacity to do so was practically impossible as opposed to a world where even when you did not want to sin you were met with diverse avenues to commit sin leaving you with no choice. That is how devastating the effect of sin on mankind was, in subjecting man to slavery and bondage.

Then in the subsequent verse, twelve, God gives Moses a token of this great deliverance

> *And He said, certainly I will be with thee and this shall be the token unto thee, that I have sent thee:* **when thou has brought the people out of Egypt ye shall serve God upon this mountain.**
>
> **Exodus 3:12**

God meant: Moses this is the sure word of prophecy gone ahead of you – when my people shall worship on this mountain of the LORD, know that that great ingathering by my hand is fulfilled (it is important to understand that God declares the end right from the beginning). In detail, God was saying, watch out for the mountain of the house of the LORD and in that time when my people shall serve me and shall not serve in Egypt (which is a typology of sin, slavery and bondage)! This mountain is what is referred to as **"the place which the Lord thy God hath chosen to place his name there."** - *(we shall look in detail what this place is in the chapter on the Mysteries of the*

Feast of Weeks). Though Israel was to remember as the significance of the Feast of Weeks that they were bondmen in Egypt yet the celebration of this Holy Convocation was to take place in the place the LORD has chosen - definitely outside of Egypt! What does this tell us? In simple language, God would signify that now I will gather you as the harvest from the fields of Egypt where you were bondmen unto Myself – the land which I promised to give unto your father Abraham the progenitor by a covenant enacting this whole agenda of redemption as free men! Thus, God is not now bringing salvation to mankind, because the grace of God that brings salvation has appeared unto all men in this present world (Titus 2:11 – 12 paraphrased). Rather, we are in the days of the massive ingathering of the harvest – the quick work of salvation has already been wrought. So it makes complete sense how simple it is for one to be saved like the Ethiopian eunuch among many others – who said "I believe that Jesus Christ is the Son God" (Acts 8:27-39) and that was it! Immediately, he was saved and got baptized. In detail, he was instantly translated from the kingdom of darkness into the Kingdom of God's dear Son Jesus Christ. His spirit which is the real person (being) was regenerated, that is born again

(Titus 3:5; John 3:3, 6). In another place we are told, as many as believed were baptized and were added unto the Church that same day! (Acts 2:41). That is how quick God has made it!! Hallelujah!!!

The Blowing of Trumpets

> *Speak unto the children of Israel, saying, In the seventh month, in the first day of the month, shall ye have a Sabbath, a memorial of blowing of trumpets, an holy convocation.*
>
> *Ye shall do no servile work therein: but ye shall offer an offering made by fire unto the Lord.*
>
> *Leviticus 23:24-25*

After the great harvest has ended, it shall be followed with the last trump.

> *Behold, I show you a mystery; We shall not all sleep, but we shall all be changed, In a moment, in the twinkling of an eye, **at the last trump: for the trumpet shall sound**, and the dead shall be raised incorruptible, and we shall be changed.*
>
> *I Corinthians 15:51-52*

*For the LORD Himself shall descend from heaven with a shout, with the voice of the archangel, and **with the trump of God**: and the dead in Christ shall rise first:*

I Thess 4:16

So this season is where we are heading towards after the Feast of Weeks has ended. And remember that we are in the climax of **the Feast of Weeks**. On the day when the trumpet shall sound, we shall rise awaiting our union with God!

The Day of Atonement

When the word "atone" first entered the English language it meant to be reconciled. It comes from the joining of the words "at" and "one" according to the Merriam Webster dictionary. For instance, to be at one with God thus conveyed the idea of the restoration of a peaceful and harmonious state between God and mankind through Jesus Christ. Scripture speaking in Leviticus twenty three verse twenty seven:

__Also on the tenth day of this seventh month there shall be a day of atonement__: it shall be an holy convocation unto you; and ye shall afflict

> *your souls, and offer an offering made by fire unto the Lord.*
>
> ***Leviticus 23:27***

On that day, the Day of Atonement, man shall be re-united with God again in literal terms. *Behold, what manner of love the Father hath bestowed upon us, that we should be called the sons of God. Beloved, now are we the sons of God, and it doth not yet appear what we shall be: but we know that,* **when He shall appear, we shall be like Him; for we shall see Him as He is.** *For* **the Lord Himself shall descend from heaven** *with a shout, with the voice of the archangel, and with the trump of God: and* **the dead in Christ shall rise first: Then we which are alive and remain shall be caught up together with them in the clouds, to meet the Lord in the air: and so shall we ever be with the Lord.** *(I John 3:1-2; I Thess 4:16-17)*

Therefore after the last trump when we are caught up with God, we shall be joined to God forever and not only that we shall be like God reigniting and fulfilling God's word – "Let us create man in our own image after our likeness *(Genesis 1:26)*". This is important to communicate that nothing of what God has said shall fall to the ground!

The Feast of Tabernacles

> *Speak unto the children of Israel, saying, the fifteenth day of this seventh month **shall be the feast of tabernacles** for seven days unto the Lord.*
>
> *Leviticus 23:34*

The feast of tabernacles is the climax of the Holy Convocations. Its perfect positioning reveals God's great intent of finishing the work of redemption in grand style. Concerning the feast of tabernacles, the whole of Israel were to live in booths seven days. In effect, all generations will know that they dwelt in ***temporary structures*** when the LORD led them out of Egypt by a mighty and an outstretched arm (Leviticus 23:42-43). To most people that was where it ended. More than that, God was revealing an eternal truth in His work of redemption. Once again it is interesting how this follows particularly, the Day of Atonement, to the end, the unveiling of a Mastermind (grand design) in the last three of the Holy Convocations such that they occur in the same collection of time and of season – the first, tenth and fifteenth day of the same time frame.

In a deeper context God was unveiling how in His work of redemption, this corrupted body which is our temporary earthly tabernacle shall finally put on immortality – a permanent tabernacle *eternal in the heavens*. It is amazing how this takes place after we are joined together with God on that Day of Atonement.

> ***For we know that if our earthly house of this tabernacle were dissolved, we have a building of God, an house not made with hands, eternal in the heavens.***
>
> *For in this we groan, earnestly desiring to be clothed upon with our house which is from heaven:*
>
> *If so be that being clothed we shall not be found naked.*
>
> *For we that are in this tabernacle do groan, being burdened: not for that we would be unclothed, but clothed upon, **that mortality might be swallowed up of life**.*
>
> *Now he that hath wrought us for the selfsame thing is God, who also hath given unto us the earnest of the Spirit.*
>
> ***2 Corinthians 5:1-5***

Wait a minute, it doesn't end there, and we shall also dwell with the LORD in permanent mansions – prepared in heaven for the redeemed!

> ***In my Father's house are many mansions****: if it were not so, I would have told you.* ***I go to prepare a place for you.*** *And if I go and prepare a place for you,* ***I will come again, and receive you unto myself; that where I am, there ye may be also.***

> *John 14:2-3*

In the book of Revelation chapter twenty-one verse three to seven we are told:

> *And I heard a great voice out of heaven saying, Behold, the tabernacle of God is with men, and he will dwell with them, and they shall be his people, and God himself shall be with them, and be their God.*

> *And God shall wipe away all tears from their eyes; and there shall be no more death, neither sorrow, nor crying, neither shall there be any more pain: for the former things are passed away.*

> *And he that sat upon the throne said, Behold, I make all things new. And he said unto me,*

write: for these words are true and faithful.

And he said unto me, It is done. I am Alpha and Omega, the beginning and the end. I will give unto him that is athirst of the fountain of the water of life freely.

He that overcometh shall inherit all things; and I will be his God, and he shall be my son.

If you pay close attention to these holy convocations they have all to do with salvation and deliverance from sin, slavery and bondage. Consequently, they were instituted to perform the prophecy spoken and restore all things bringing man to his original estate which he in times past lost to the devil. A good understanding of these is important to prepare the believer (the Church) to war a good warfare in fulfilment of the prophecy spoken!

Chapter two

The Mysteries of the Feast of Weeks

Everything about God is a mystery! The wisdom of God is communicated in mysteries (I Cor 2:7)!! It is the sole reason the natural mind cannot appreciate the things of God and until one is granted access to understand, they do not deliver. I mean, how do you multiply five loaves and two fishes to feed five thousand men just by a prayer of thanksgiving and how do you call a man who has been dead, embalmed and buried for four days to come out from the dead and it is delivered as expected! As these examples are common to us and we have seen them repeated in our days especially the latter, the same is true for all the other mysteries of God and in our case the delivery of the mysteries of the Feast of Weeks. We are in the days of mysteries!!!

Follow as we look closely at Deuteronomy chapter sixteen verse nine and ten

Seven weeks shalt thou number unto thee: begin to number the seven weeks from such time as thou beginnest to put the sickle to the corn.

And thou shalt KEEP THE FEAST OF WEEKS unto the Lord thy God with a tribute of a freewill offering of thine hand, which thou shalt give unto the Lord thy God, according as the Lord thy God hath blessed thee:

And thou shalt rejoice before the Lord thy God, thou, and thy son, and thy daughter, and thy manservant, and thy maidservant, and the Levite that is within thy gates, and the stranger, and the fatherless, and the widow, that are among you, in the place which the Lord thy God hath chosen to place his name there.

And thou shalt remember that thou was a bondman in Egypt: and thou shalt observe and do these statutes.

Deuteronomy 16:9-12

Now let us consider the hidden themes of the feast.

"...to put the sickle to the corn."

To put the sickle to the corn is symbolic of the time of the harvest. Take note that the Holy Convocations up until The Feast of Weeks were all leading to the ingathering of the harvest of the souls of men. In the fourth chapter of John's gospel verse thirty five through to forty one (paraphrased); Jesus said:

> ***Say not ye, there are yet four months, and then cometh harvest?*** *Behold, I say unto you, lift up your eyes, and look on the fields;* **FOR THEY ARE WHITE ALREADY TO HARVEST**

> *...And many of* **THE SAMARITANS OF THAT CITY BELIEVED ON HIM** *for the saying of the woman, which testified, He told me all that ever I did.*

> *...And* **MANY MORE BELIEVED** *because of his own word;*

Jesus categorically clarified the times – don't say the time of the harvest is not yet. Look on the fields, the sickle has been put to the corn already alluding to the prophecy - ***begin to number the seven weeks from such time as thou begin to put the sickle to the***

corn. Additionally, from this passage of scripture, Jesus referred to the souls of the Samaritans as the harvest in the fields. In comparison therefore with ***"...as thou beginnest to put the sickle to the corn."***, God in his infinite wisdom was not speaking of the harvest of corn or wheat or whatever the people of Israel cultivated but the souls of men and for that matter in this very dispensation – the last days. Is this just a coincidence? Well we can confirm this from Matthew's gospel chapter nine verse thirty five to thirty eight:

> *And Jesus went about all the cities and villages, teaching in their synagogues, and preaching the gospel of the kingdom, and healing every sickness and every disease AMONG THE PEOPLE.*

> *But when HE SAW THE MULTITUDES, he was moved with compassion on them, because they fainted, and were scattered abroad, as sheep having no shepherd.*

> *Then saith he unto his disciples, THE HARVEST truly is plenteous, but the labourers are few;*

> ***Pray ye therefore the Lord of the harvest that he will send forth labourers into his harvest.***
>
> *Matt 9:35-38*

Jesus saw the multitudes and referred to them as "the harvest"! He didn't see wheat or corn rather He saw the multitudes!! And so there we have it. God has in several places referred to the souls of men as the harvest. Now let me quickly add that the Old Testament is a concealed book of the New Testament. Thus it contains many hidden themes which are revealed in the New Testament.

> ***"...as thou beginnest to put the sickle to the corn."***

This portion of scripture is to mean "before you put the sickle to the corn". That is, prior to the ingathering of the harvest, make preparation for harvest. Every farmer knows this very well as well as its relevance to post-harvest season. For instance when silos are not properly prepared for storage of the grains, it could cause very serious post-harvest loses. Again, God in His infinite wisdom commands that before the harvest is brought in, certain preparations be made. What are these preparations then?

"Seven weeks shalt thou number unto thee: begin to number the seven weeks from such time as thou beginnest to put the sickle to the corn."

Interesting! Just number seven weeks? What was God thinking, you may ask? We are expected to bring in the harvest (souls), the magnitude of which has never been perceived before and all that God, the Author of wisdom, says we should do as preparation is to count seven weeks (seven sevens since a week is another set of seven)! Exactly!! That's all God wants us to do for the preparation; just count, as He would do for Himself what His mouth has spoken. Alright, so we are going to count together. Are you ready? To help us count will be Apostle Matthew from the first chapter of his gospel verse seventeen

So all the generations from Abraham to David are fourteen generations; and from David until the carrying away into Babylon are fourteen generations; and from the carrying away into Babylon unto Christ are fourteen generations.

Matt 1:17

Now let's take a simple pictorial view of this scripture:

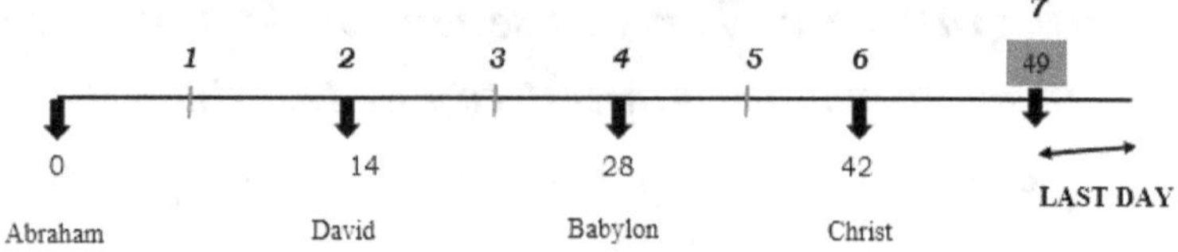

Thus counting from Abraham to Christ are forty two generations. This makes six sevens, meaning one more seven is needed to complete the count of seven sevens. What then is this last seven? Well, let's find out.

Now Scripture has provided several evidence to that effect seeing that God has never left Himself without a witness (*Acts 14:17a*). We shall consider two of these evidence in brief. Let us understand that the last seven runs directly into the LAST DAY which is the fiftieth day (*Even unto the morrow after the seventh Sabbath shall ye number fifty days; ... Lev 23:16*). That is to mean, the last seven ends at the start of the LAST DAY. Indirectly, you can determine the end of the seventh seven when you identify the start of the LAST DAY. Let's take a look at the following scriptures to verify the beginning of the LAST DAY thus the end of the seventh seven to complete the count.

Evidence one:

SEVEN WEEKS SHALT THOU NUMBER UNTO THEE: begin to number the seven weeks from such time as thou beginnest to put the sickle to the corn.

And thou shalt keep the feast of weeks unto the Lord thy God with a tribute of a freewill offering of thine hand, which thou shalt give unto the Lord thy God, according as the Lord thy God hath blessed thee:

Deut 16:9-10

And ye shall count unto you from the morrow after the sabbath, from the day that ye brought the sheaf of the wave offering; seven sabbaths shall be complete:

EVEN UNTO THE MORROW AFTER THE SEVENTH SABBATH shall ye number fifty days; and ye shall offer a new meat offering unto the Lord.

Lev 23:15-16

But this is that which was spoken by the prophet Joel;

> *And it shall come to pass in THE LAST DAYS, saith God, I WILL POUR OUT OF MY SPIRIT UPON ALL FLESH: and your sons and your daughters shall prophesy, and your young men shall see visions, and your old men shall dream dreams:*
>
> *And on my servants and on my handmaidens I will pour out in those days of my Spirit; and they shall prophesy:*
>
> *Acts 2:16-18*

According to *Lev 23:15-16,* the people of Israel were to number **plus one** to the seven sevens making **fifty** in all. Thus the fiftieth coincided with the LAST DAY. Moreover, in *Acts 2:16-18,* the LAST DAY shall be marked by the out pour of the Holy Spirit *upon ALL FLESH.* Before this time, the Holy Spirit came upon only a select people but in the description we see sons and daughters, young men and old men, servants and handmaidens. That is to say, when you shall see the Holy Spirit come upon all men know that it is the LAST DAY! This totally distinguished from what used to be known. Therefore, the LAST DAY is that which began at Jerusalem in the upper room when the Holy Spirit who is the Promise of the Father was given to all who were gathered together even including the women that were with them (*Acts 1:14-15*).

> *And, being assembled together with them, commanded them that they should not depart from JERUSALEM, but wait for the promise of the Father, which, saith he, ye have heard of me.*

> *For John truly baptized with water; but ye shall be baptized with the Holy Ghost not many days hence.*

> *Acts 1:4-5*

> *And THEY WERE ALL FILLED WITH THE HOLY GHOST, and began to speak with other tongues, as the Spirit gave them utterance.*

> *Acts 2:4*

By inference, the seventh seven is the generation from Christ to the day just before the out pour of the Holy Ghost on the day of Pentecost.

Evidence two:

> *And it shall come to pass IN THE LAST DAYS, that THE MOUNTAIN OF THE LORD'S HOUSE shall be established in the top of the mountains,*

> *and shall be exalted above the hills; and ALL NATIONS SHALL FLOW UNTO IT.*
>
> *AND MANY PEOPLE shall go and say, Come ye, and let us go up to the mountain of the Lord, to the house of the God of Jacob; and HE WILL TEACH US OF HIS WAYS, AND WE WILL WALK IN HIS PATHS: for out of Zion shall go forth the law, and the word of the Lord from Jerusalem.*
>
> *Isa 2:2-3*

We shall carefully examine this evidence in the light of other scriptures to ascertain its veracity concerning the LAST DAY and by inference the seventh seven.

a. IN THE LAST DAYS

Again we see another use of the phrase "LAST DAYS". Isaiah in his prophecy speaks concerning the LAST DAYS even at the time between the generation of David and the carrying away into Babylon (Matt 1:17). The Prophet lived in the days of Kings Uzziah, Jotham, Ahaz and Hezekiah (Isa 1:1) and that is considered to be some 700 years before Christ. What is more, the LAST DAYS is not during the days of Christ but after the days of Christ (see calendar on pg. 42) and that is a very long duration to predict any happenings with such detail. So to have had a prophecy such as this can only mean the hand of God at work. What were Isaiah's prophecies?

b. *THE MOUNTAIN OF THE LORD'S HOUSE*

Now I want to draw two distinctions here; the mountain of the LORD and the house on the mountain of the LORD otherwise, the mountain of the LORD's house.

The mountain of the LORD is what is referred to as Jerusalem according to Zechariah chapter eight verse three:

> *Thus saith the Lord; I am returned unto Zion, and will dwell in the midst of Jerusalem: and JERUSALEM SHALL BE CALLED A CITY OF TRUTH; AND THE MOUNTAIN OF THE LORD of hosts the holy mountain.*
>
> *Zech 8:3*

Jesus Christ knowing the prophecy foretold and its relevance to God's move of the ingathering in these last days, before His ascension, commanded the disciples not to depart from Jerusalem (Acts 1:4).

> *And, being assembled together with them,* **commanded them that they should not depart from Jerusalem,** *but wait for the promise of the Father, which, saith he, ye have heard of me.*
>
> *Acts 1:4*

This was a clear instruction. Perhaps the disciples did not understand the purpose at the time but as prophecy unfolded before their eyes all became clear as it is even much clearer to us now. There again, this is clear indication of a master plan confirming God's capacity to do what He has spoken to do concerning the ingathering of the harvest – the feast of weeks!

Thus, the house on the mountain of the LORD would be the Church in Jerusalem. Why is that? In I Timothy 3:15, we see the Church referred to as the house of God.

> *...* **the house of God, which is the church of the living God,** *the pillar and ground of the truth.*
>
> *I Timothy 3:15*

So we could reason to say the LAST DAY shall officially begin at the Church in JERUSALEM according to Isaiah chapter two verse two, Zechariah chapter eight verse three and First Timothy chapter three verse fifteen. However, remember that in Jesus' own words, this Church movement will start in Jerusalem but shall go on to the outermost part of the earth. And this is evident today on the earth – the Church of God has gone and continues to spread to every part of the world including strong Islamic nations and Communist nations.

> *But ye shall receive power, after that the Holy Ghost is come upon you: and ye shall be witnesses unto me both **in Jerusalem, and in all Judaea, and in Samaria, and unto the uttermost part of the earth***
>
> *Acts 1:8*

c. ALL NATIONS SHALL FLOW UNTO IT

Another very striking thing Isaiah predicts should take place on the LAST DAY beginning in Jerusalem (now that we've proven *THE MOUNTAIN OF THE LORD'S HOUSE* to mean the Church in Jerusalem) is that every nation shall be gathered in Jerusalem on that day. Wow, that's unimaginable, isn't it? Can I tell you this; that would certainly take God to fulfil! That is to mean, on the day you shall see all nations under heaven at the time, gather in Jerusalem, know this that the LAST DAY has begun! Did it happen as prophesied? Let's look at Acts chapter two verse four through to five.

> ***And they were all filled with the Holy Ghost, and began to speak with other tongues, as the Spirit gave them utterance.***
>
> ***AND THERE WERE DWELLING AT JERUSALEM JEWS, DEVOUT MEN, OUT OF EVERY NATION UNDER HEAVEN.***
>
> *Acts 2:4-5*

"And there were dwelling men out of every nation under heaven!" So there we have it... On this day, every nation gathered in Jerusalem to mark the beginning of the LAST DAY

d. *AND MANY PEOPLE ...HE WILL TEACH US OF HIS WAYS, AND WE WILL WALK IN HIS PATHS*

Another sign the Prophet says shall mark the LAST DAY will be that the word of the LORD will be taught from Jerusalem and many people will respond to this WORD. That is to say, many will accept this WORD. So when you shall see unprecedented number of souls come to the LORD out of every nation, know for sure, it is the LAST DAY! So we examine the fulfilment of this prophecy in Acts chapter two verse fourteen through to forty one.

> *But Peter, standing up with the eleven, lifted up his voice, and said unto them, Ye men of Judaea, and all ye that dwell at Jerusalem, be this known unto you, and HEARKEN TO MY WORDS:*
>
> *Now when they heard this, THEY WERE PRICKED IN THEIR HEART, AND SAID UNTO PETER AND TO THE REST OF THE APOSTLES, MEN AND BRETHREN, WHAT SHALL WE DO?*
>
> *Then they that gladly received his word were baptized: and THE SAME DAY THERE WERE ADDED UNTO THEM ABOUT THREE THOUSAND SOULS.*
>
> *Acts 2:14, 37, 41*

So according to the scripture above, we identify that the WORD of the LORD came to many people who had come from all over the world and were gathered in Jerusalem. In the end, about three thousand people were saved and added to the disciples.

So to confirm the LAST DAY will mean to have all these predictions happen at the same time. After examining the predictions of the LAST DAY as prophesied by the prophet Isaiah, we can conclude to say all the evidence presented in the books of Zechariah and Acts fits what took place on that day at Jerusalem in the upper room when the Holy Spirit who is the Promise of the Father was given to all who were gathered together even including the women that were with them (*Acts 1:14-15*). By inference, the seventh seven to complete the count as commanded by God as preparation for the feast, ended just before the happenings fulfilled in the book of Acts (Acts 2:1).

Thus to complete the count of seven sevens will be to number from Abraham to the generation just before the out pour of the Holy Spirit   (see calendar below)

However, one other important question arises and other proofs which will validate the mysteries of the Feast of Weeks and for that matter the delivery of the mysteries in our days especially concerning the Church!

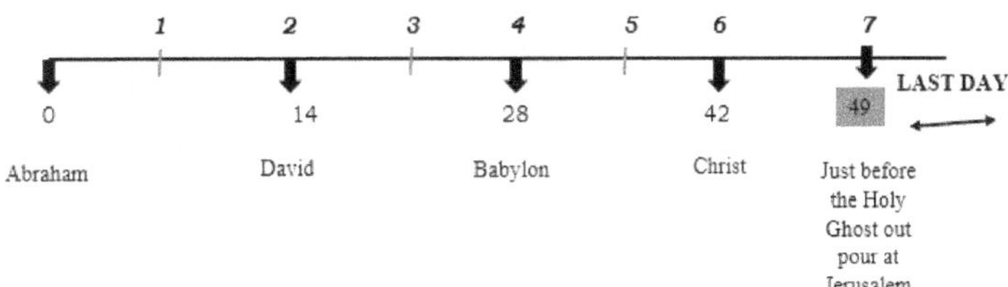

Why is the count from Abraham and not Adam the first man?

It is of utmost importance to answer this question as it strengthens the validity of the mystery especially its relevance in our days – the Last days! Yes, in the events after the fall when God drove Adam from the Garden of Eden, He announced his work of redemption (*And I will put enmity between thee and the woman, and between thy seed and her seed; it shall bruise thy head, and thou shalt bruise his heel. Gen 3:15*) yet He dealt with man on an individual basis. In Genesis chapter four, we see that in the process of time Cain and Abel came to worship with their offerings. We know the story; Abel's offering was accepted of God but Cain's rejected. Then God said to Cain; "if you do well, that is, do what is right and you will be accepted." In the course of time men began to call on the name of God (Genesis 4:26). Yet God never chose a man out of his kindred by whom He will raise for Himself a people that will eventually be the lineage through which Jesus Christ, the seed of the woman, would come to finish and perfect the work of redemption remedying sin and its consequence forever except Abraham. Thus the LORD established His covenant with him and his seed forever (Genesis 12,17). We see same confirmed:

> ***Now to Abraham and his seed were the promises made. He saith not, And to seeds, as of many; but as of one, And to thy seed, which is Christ.***
>
> *Galatians 3:16*

Therefore, the blueprint to redemption must start with Abraham and end in Christ. All, from Adam to before Abraham, God dealt with on a one-on-one basis.

This Generation Shall Not Pass

> *Verily I say unto you, **This** generation shall not pass, till all these things be fulfilled.*
>
> *Matt 24:34*

It is a perfect and a beautiful thing to behold the detail of God's plan especially when you discover how these pieces from different parts of scripture over varying ages and generations fit together all pointing to our God and His wisdom – how unsearchable and His ways past finding out! In Matthew's gospel, repeated in Mark and Luke's gospel, chapter twenty four and verse thirty four Jesus Christ makes a revealing statement – This generation shall not pass, till all these things be fulfilled. At first sight, you may consider that Jesus Christ spoke to the people that lived during His days here on earth and maybe just some few years for those who lived after His death and resurrection. But it's been a whole over two thousand years and it doesn't seem it is ending sooner. There again, how unsearchable is God's wisdom!

Of course Jesus Christ meant more than what it looked like superficially. Keep in mind that Jesus Christ came at the start of the seventh set of the seven generations and exited just before the end of the seventh set of the seven generations. A generation is not necessarily determined by the number of years but by the dynamics of God's agenda. At the time Jesus Christ made this statement, He was getting ready to go to the cross, resurrect and exit the scene in the flesh ending the long run of the seventh set of the seven generations consequently ushering in the Holy Ghost to begin the fiftieth day which is the last day generation. It is in light of this that Jesus Christ prophetically makes this bold statement – ***"This generation shall not pass, till all these things be fulfilled"***. The generation he made reference to was the fiftieth day generation which is the last on the calendar. The exact duration of this generation is not given to us to know but the sign for the generation He has given us to know – for it is not for us to know the times and seasons which the Father has put in His own power but it shall be after that the Holy Ghost has come upon you (Acts 1:7-8 paraphrased).

Therefore the fiftieth day which is the LAST DAY of the Feast of Weeks is the same as the LAST DAY predicted by the prophet Isaiah and fulfilled in the book of Acts (Acts 2).

In The Place Which The Lord Thy God Hath Chosen To Place His Name There.

One other supporting proof to the full delivery of the mystery of the Feast of Weeks is the place the LORD has chosen to place His name (Deut. 16:11). Again, this is very important as it narrows on the details of the prophecy foretold. In other words, before this prophecy of the mystery of the Feast of Weeks could be fulfilled (remember we have said that the purpose of this is for the ingathering of the harvest of the souls of men), God had to specifically choose Jerusalem out of the many cities of Israel. A failure in this part of prophecy would crumble God's redemptive agenda. And there we see it come to pass:

> ***...this city Jerusalem which I have chosen, and the house of which I said, My name shall be there.***
>
> ***II Kings 23:27b***
>
> ***...in Jerusalem, the city which the Lord did choose out of all the tribes of Israel, to put his name there***
>
> ***I Kings 14:21***

Thus, God has been conscious to fulfill all that was prophesied. The relevance of this is, first it commits the ingathering of the harvest agenda in full force and second, reassures that the God who spoke concerning these things in times past and performed them will also perfect what is remaining. We shall see prophecies of the ingathering of the harvest of the souls of men fulfilled before our very eyes! Amen!!

The Pentecost

> *And when the day of Pentecost was fully come, they were all with one accord in one place.*
>
> *And they were all filled with the Holy Ghost, and began to speak with other tongues, as the Spirit gave them utterance.*
>
> *Acts 2:1,4*

By this time, when the day of Pentecost (fiftieth) was finally come, the preparation being completed, "the sickle could then be put to the corn". And God demonstrated this by sending the Holy Ghost, unveiling the mystery of tongues speaking. This was new. The kind has never been such that when the people heard it, they marveled saying 'we do hear them speak in our tongues the wonderful works of God'. (Acts 2:7,11 paraphrased). It is intriguing that all God did was to unveil the mystery of tongues after the preparation for the ingathering of the harvest. Perhaps, it would have been easier to relate if we saw angels with drawn swords destroying devils, sin and everything that stood in the way or like Israel would have expected, a great army of men that would conquer the enemy in the way – an unstoppable army! Rather we see God introduce a heavenly language – tongues! You may ask; is this enough for the unprecedented work of the last days? But can I tell you this, God is a master strategist who knows what to do to get every other thing done and you can be rest assured that resident in the mystery of tongues speaking is God's wisdom and power to get the work done! Don't forget that on that same day the mystery was unveiled, it drew the multitudes out of which 3,000 souls were saved and added to the disciples that same day (Acts 2:6,41)!

God's Wisdom – Speaking With Other Tongues

Never take lightly the many sided wisdom of God (Eph 3:10)! Never ever dare thrash any facet of the varying wisdom of God into the bin. Because, this is God's arsenal to reveal His Church especially in this dispensation of the last days. Hear this, you can't achieve what God has planned to do on the earth beneath and the heaven above with your earthy or intellectual wisdom! Let the Church be warned!! This many sided wisdom of God is from above and therefore above all!!! (Jam 3:17)

Now, one of the many sides of the wisdom of God that marked the beginning of the last days dispensation understanding from scripture that the seventh-seven ended just when the Holy Ghost was given (see calendar on pg. 53) is the WISDOM OF SPEAKING IN TONGUES.

Clearly, this wisdom of God for the last days' dispensation has more or less been misunderstood. Otherwise, the dynamic magnitude of proofs it should have produced would surpass what it currently appears to be. What would happen if this wisdom of God were fully exploited? While most of the Catholics and Orthodox believers if not all have thought lightly of this wisdom either as considering it to have ceased to operate or explained it away to mean just the talent or ability to speak so many languages of men, the majority of the Pentecostals and Charismatics have somewhat considered it to be a feeling of rattling some phoneme and that ends it. No! That's far from it. Rather, this is amongst the many sided wisdom of God for the last days dispensation designed to climax God's harvest calendar. The enormity of its power is overwhelming.

The Creation Story

In Genesis chapter one when God created the heavens and the earth we understand that God only spoke to bring into being the magnificence we see in the world today even in its corrupted state. Therefore you can imagine the splendor and beauty of God's creation before the corruption. Meanwhile all this glory was not by any of those sophisticated construction equipment we see in our world today but by WORDS – "and God said…".

However, have you taken time to know what tongue God spoke at creation? Does it really matter to know; we have Genesis chapter one translated into English and other tongues from the original Hebrew script as given to Moses so of what use is it, one may ask? Considering that at the time God delivered the Pentateuch to Moses He had already divided the people into different languages, it was reasonable to communicate with Moses who is a Jew in the Hebrew tongue. However, it is worth mentioning why God did so. In the account in Genesis chapter eleven reading from verse one through to nine, we understand that the whole earth was of one language after the flood and so they sought to build themselves a tower that could reach heaven. God seeing what they had imagined to do and were already doing, in His infinite wisdom chose to stop them from the evil by confounding their tongue so that they could no longer understand one another. Therefore a project as huge as the "creation" of the tower of Babel was defeated by "tongues". This underpins the place of tongues in "creation" and for that matter why what tongue God spoke at creation or speaks is of great importance. An extension to this is even how things that did not exist anywhere responded to "...and God said" "...and God saw" at creation. Then, what language could God had spoken for which they heard and obeyed – for He called those things that be not as though they were (Rom 4:17).

> ***And the Spirit of God moved... and God said... and God saw***
>
> ***Gen 1:2-4***

Therefore the wisdom of God is this "the Spirit has moved (this begun on the day of Pentecost), so speak the tongue!"

Adam The Son Of God

In Luke's gospel chapter three verse thirty eight we see a narrative of Adam as the direct son of God:

> *Which was the son of Enos, which was the son of Seth, which was the son of **Adam, which was the son of God.***
>
> ***Luke 3:38***

Before I go on, let me provoke you with this question:

Before the fall where God would come down in the day and commune with Adam, what tongue/language did God speak?

In Genesis, after God had created most things, He climaxed His creation by introducing a god-man (Psa 82:6, John 10:34). There's never been anything of the sort, never! In detail, God introduced a being into the Godhead – to be like God, to like what God likes and have power and dominion on earth as God in heaven (Gen 1:26). God proved this when He brought every beast of the earth and every fowl of the air to Adam to see what he would call them and whatever Adam called every creature, that was forever established (Genesis 2:19). So Adam was the god in flesh. It is no surprise that Jesus Christ in whom dwells all the fullness of the Godhead bodily - the God in flesh - is referred to as the Last Adam (1 Cor 15:45) and in other places is contrasted with Adam on the subject of righteousness and sin, life and death among others (Rom 5:15, 1 Cor 15:22).

Like every Father, God prepared a special place for Adam to live comfortably (Garden of Eden) and ensured that Adam had every provision. But most important of the things God provided was a strong communication. God talked with His god-son – Adam! There again, this was something never heard of. The striking part of this phenomenon is that the god-son spoke in the language of the Godhead. *As a direct son of God, Adam before the fall spoke the tongue of God – his Father!* It is "supernaturally" as natural, where a son took on the traits of the Father including the tongue of the Father. This however was before the fall of Adam, where there was no veil between the courts, neither did he require any medium to speak with God nor had to be enabled externally to carry out that use – it was inherent. This was the situation in the beginning; there was no exact distinction between the two realms – the supernatural and the natural.

Consequently, Adam bare a son in his own corrupted image. Back to the tongue Adam spoke, that was the tongue of God. Adam spoke in the tongue of God as he reigned on earth as the god of the earth. It was by this tongue he kept the creation in control as mandated by God. By this tongue, the host of creation had respect unto their god – Adam. All things worked together for good like the narrative about the man set under authority who *says* to one 'go' and he goes, 'come' and he comes, 'do this' and it is exactly done (Luke 7:8). What a joy it was at the time! It is in this light that Jesus Christ calls the redeemed back into the place of the original tongue as seen in Mark's gospel chapter sixteen verse seventeen:

> *And these signs shall follow* **them that believe;** **In my name** *shall they cast out devils;* **they shall speak with new tongues;**
>
> **Mark 16:17**

"...them that believe in my name shall speak with new tongues! Hallelujah, Glory to God!"

And in the Acts of the Apostles chapter two verses four we read:

> *And they were all filled with the Holy Ghost and BEGAN TO SPEAK WITH OTHER TONGUES AS THE SPIRIT GAVE THEM UTTERANCE.*

For the first time since Adam, we see men access this realm again – the tongue of God as the Holy Spirit gave them utterance.

All of this happening on the fiftieth day of the feast – the last day!! What a time to be alive and a generation to be a part of – marking moments of God's eternal plan to climax His work of redemption here on earth!!!

The Apostle Paul's Encounter

In 2 Corinthians chapter twelve reading from verse two through to six, the Apostle Paul describes an experience where he was caught up into the third heavens and there he heard such unspeakable words that cannot or should not be uttered (that should draw our minds to Romans 8:26 which we should consider in a moment). In other words, Paul heard certain unknown tongues which is spoken in the third heaven – the tongues of God. In this place, Paul seeks to draw the believer to realms beyond this natural and what happens there. This is where the Apostle Paul comes in by revelation to answer in 2 Corinthians 12:2-4 to say there is a language in heaven and spoken by God and he was privileged to hear them. And what he heard he compares to unspeakable words or as it were, there is not any tongue of this natural to match. It is not surprising therefore that in Paul's testimony he thanked God that he speaks in tongues more than all at Corinth (I Cor 14:18). Now this same apostle as by the inspiration of the Holy Spirit writes about a certain unspeakable language given us by the Holy Spirit in Romans chapter eight verse twenty-six (we shall later consider that in detail).

That could suggest to mean that God communicated with men in the language of men and when He had to communicate with the God-head, He did so with an unknown tongue. This unknown tongue can be said to be the tongue of God and only understood by God.

Let's take a closer look at these scriptures:

> *26 Likewise the Spirit also helpeth our infirmities: for we **KNOW NOT** what we should pray for as we **OUGHT**: but the Spirit Himself maketh intercession for us with **GROANINGS** which cannot be **UTTERED**.*

> [27] *And he that searcheth the hearts **KNOWETH** what is the mind of the Spirit, because he maketh intercession for the saints according to the **WILL OF GOD**.*
>
> [28] *And we **KNOW THAT ALL THINGS** work together for good to them that love **GOD**, to them who are the called according to his purpose.*
>
> **Romans 8:26-28**

These scriptures tell of the intricacies of tongues speaking which is evident of the infilling of the Holy Ghost (Act 2:4).

The first thing to note here is the limitation of the human or natural mind to comprehend the depths of the supernatural, and as a result, the inability to appreciate or express same in communion with God especially in prayer. Let me emphasize that God at every point in time has what we ought to pray about which may not be available to the human or natural mind.

It is with regards to this that God the Father appoints the ministry of the Holy Spirit. The Holy Spirit is our one and only access to the supernatural/spiritual. I mean His name – Spirit – explicitly defines His work.

He launches the born-again believer to explore the supernatural (John 3:6). Not only that, He teaches the born-again believer the way of the supernatural and in our case prayer (John 14:26).

However, after the Spirit of GOD teaches the life of the supernatural, it is the sole responsibility of the believer to manifest what is learnt from the spiritual into the physical - the Holy Spirit makes intercession for us with groaning which cannot be **UTTERED!**

So let's take a case study from the book of the Acts of the Apostles chapter two and verse four:

> *And they were all filled with the Holy Ghost, and **began to speak with other tongues,** as the Spirit gave them **utterance.***
>
> ***Acts 2:4***

I hope you see what I am saying but let's look at it together. In Romans chapter eight, the twenty-sixth verse, those intercessions made by the Holy Ghost could not be uttered. Why? This is because, it is not the responsibility of the Holy Ghost to do the speaking or express in the physical (speaking in this situation is a physical dimension). We see a confirmation in this regard – the Holy Ghost gave that utterance to the believers who were gathered in the upper room on the day of Pentecost and then they (believers) began to speak! So that, that which could not be uttered could now be heard from the mouth of the believers.

Every unspeakable utterance in the spiritual realm are made 'speakable' and hearable to cause a response in the natural realm by the mystery of tongues speaking. And also remember that we live in a world that was created by the WORD and being upheld by the WORD of His power (Gen 1, Heb 1:3) and that all there is, he called them and they came into being (Rom 4:17). So the importance of tongues cannot be overemphasized. For in many things we err if not all things. If any man errs not in **WORD**, the same is perfect, and able also to control the whole universe (James 3:2 paraphrased). Everything there is and can ever be is by tongues – this one is God's wisdom!

Juxtaposing 2 Corinthians 12:2-4 and Romans 8:26 will mean the unspeakable word or language Paul heard when he was caught up in the third heaven, which is the original language/mode of command by God, is what is now given to believers by the

Holy Spirit. This is what is confirmed as speaking in unknown tongues as the Spirit gave utterance!

This mystery of speaking in tongues is what drew and gathered the people into the upper room area for such an unprecedented feat by the disciples on the day of Pentecost. This continued to extents where whole cities gathered (Acts 13:44). It is very important to note that God has put this wisdom in this dispensation as He rounds up the work of the ingathering in Jesus Christ by the Church. It therefore behooves on us as custodians of this mystery to fully exploit for maximum delivery. If all the beauty of the world is as a result of the unspeakable words, tongues, then you can imagine the 'explosion' when believers fully lay hold on this mystery. Remember if God put it in there, then it must be of great importance for our efficiency in fulfillment of the prophecy according to Isaiah 2:2-4.

The Lord Shall Utter His Voice Before His Army

> And **the Lord shall utter His voice** before His army: for His camp is very great: **for He is strong that executeth His word**: for **the**

> ***day of the Lord*** *is great and very terrible; and who can abide it?*
>
> ***Joel 2:11***

It is interesting to note that God has ordained the mystery of tongues speaking in accomplishing what is explained to mean the day of the LORD. How? The book of Joel chapter two verse eleven reveals that yet again - ***the Lord shall utter his voice...*** His voice is explained to mean what God says. However, paying attention to the word **"utter"** as used in this verse of the Old Testament reminds us of the same word as used in Romans chapter eight verse twenty six - *but the Spirit Himself maketh intercession for us with groanings which cannot be **uttered**.* Comparing these two statements of scripture, we can establish the mystery of tongues speaking. The effect of this mystery is sequel to the prophecy of Joel – it will stir a great awakening of the people and they shall turn unto the LORD with all their heart, with fasting and weeping and mourning. The people shall call a solemn feast like the Feast of Weeks. He says, behold the LORD shall send corn, and wine, and oil, and we shall be satisfied therewith. Corn, Wine and Oil are symbols of the flesh of Jesus Christ, the Blood of Jesus

Christ and the Holy Ghost respectively. This is the sign of the feast!

12 Therefore also now, saith the Lord, turn ye even to me with all your heart, and with fasting, and with weeping, and with mourning:

13 And rend your heart, and not your garments, and turn unto the Lord your God: for he is gracious and merciful, slow to anger, and of great kindness, and repenteth Him of the evil.

14 Who knoweth if He will return and repent, and leave a blessing behind Him; even a meat offering and a drink offering unto the Lord your God?

15 Blow the trumpet in Zion, sanctify a fast, call a solemn assembly:

*16 **Gather the people**, sanctify the congregation, assemble the elders, **gather the children, and those that suck the breasts**: let the bridegroom go forth of his chamber, and the bride out of her closet.*

17 Let the priests, the ministers of the Lord, weep between the porch and the altar, and let them say, Spare thy people, O Lord, and give not thine heritage to reproach, that the heathen should rule over them: wherefore should they say among the people, Where is their God?

[18] Then will the Lord be jealous for his land, and pity his people.

[19] Yea, the Lord will answer and say unto his people, Behold, I will send you corn, and wine, and oil, and ye shall be satisfied therewith: and I will no more make you a reproach among the heathen:

[20] But I will remove far off from you the northern army, and will drive him into a land barren and desolate, with his face toward the east sea, and his hinder part toward the utmost sea, and his stink shall come up, and his ill savour shall come up, because he hath done great things.

[21] Fear not, O land; be glad and rejoice: for the Lord will do great things.

[22] Be not afraid, ye beasts of the field: for the pastures of the wilderness do spring, for the tree beareth her fruit, the fig tree and the vine do yield their strength.

Joel 2:12-22

Prior to this moment will be that the LORD will send the rain of the Holy Ghost not moderately like we saw in the days of old, but in full in these last days of the feast. He ends this prophecy which is ordained for this last day of the feast with the great and mighty hand of God which shall culminate in great restoration, wonders and the salvation of souls.

23 Be glad then, ye children of Zion, and rejoice in the Lord your God: **for He hath given you the former rain moderately, and He will cause to come down for you the rain, the former rain, and the latter rain** *in the first month.*

24 And the floors shall be full of wheat, and the vats shall overflow with wine and oil.

25 And I will restore to you the years that the locust hath eaten, the cankerworm, and the caterpillar, and the palmerworm, my great army which I sent among you.

26 And ye shall eat in plenty, and be satisfied, and praise the name of the Lord your God, that hath dealt wondrously with you: and my people shall never be ashamed.

27 And ye shall know that I am in the midst of Israel, and that I am the Lord your God, and none else: and my people shall never be ashamed.

*28 **And it shall come to pass afterward, that I will pour out my spirit upon all flesh; and your sons and your daughters shall prophesy, your old men shall dream dreams, your young men shall see visions:***

*29 **And also upon the servants and upon the handmaids in those days will I pour out my spirit.***

30 And I will shew wonders in the heavens and in the earth, blood, and fire, and pillars of smoke.

31 The sun shall be turned into darkness, and the moon into blood, before the great and terrible day of the Lord come.

*32 **And it shall come to pass, that whosoever shall call on the name of the Lord shall be delivered: for in mount Zion and in Jerusalem shall be deliverance, as the Lord hath said, and in the remnant whom the Lord shall call.***

Joel 2:23-32

So there we see it. If God who gave the mystery of tongues speaking gave it not in any of the generations before but the last day generation, then He must have a definite purpose for it. This is no mere coincidence – it's a divine plan well crafted. Thus it is that time to awake and pick up this arsenal directed at the ingathering agenda for the times! We are privileged to be a part of an eternal agenda. Begin to blast the heavenly tongues. Inherent in the mystery of tongues speaking is everything required for the full delivery of the ingathering agenda of the Feast of Weeks. Chief or foundational of that is the all power required to get all things to work together for good, and in the end, deliver that which has been foretold. The mystery of tongues speaking taps into the 'all-power' for the delivery of the ingathering agenda. And you shall receive your 'all-power' when the Holy Ghost comes upon you then you shall be my witnesses in Jerusalem, in Judea, Samaria, and unto the utmost part of the earth. 'All-power' to reach all persons in every part of the earth!

Chapter three

The Vision and Mission Statement of Jesus Christ

The Vision Statement

The place of all-power defined Jesus Christ's vision and mission on earth underlining the relevance of the times - the pursuit of the agenda of massive ingathering of the harvest. There is nothing new to God as far as He is concerned though to men there may. Everything that has been and will be is either a result of God's perfect plan or the consequence of sin by man's action. I have heard people ask that if God who is all knowing saw before time that Adam would sin and bring all these curses we see in the world upon mankind, then why did He not stop it? I suppose that we have heard several responses to that frequently asked question including- God gave man free will to choose and God would be unjust to impose on man so Adam made His choice. And that's absolute but the angle I would like us to consider in this book as we move along is this – that in the midst of all that, God had a plan and this plan has been before the foundations of the earth were laid. The whole of that plan is founded on the bold vision statement spelt by Jesus Christ:

> *And I, if I be lifted up from the earth, will draw all men unto me.*
>
> *John 12:32*

As succinct and lucid as this statement of scripture may look, it is the foundation of the perfectly carved, detailed and the most long term plan ever been. It is worth noting that planning is one very difficult task especially in a free-willed world where every character is entitled to what they choose directly or indirectly and much more when you would have to consider the same plan through different eras, ages, generations and times yet have the plan work – and that's exactly what God in His infinite wisdom did! So you can join me say to the devil anytime and anywhere he shows up portraying to be in the lead that "GOD

HAS A PLAN!!!", hallelujah, glory to God. This plan is such that God tells Habakkuk that if He told what and how He would accomplish it, Habakkuk wouldn't believe it (Habakkuk 1:5).

Now let us consider some aspect of the plan:

And I, if I be lifted up from the earth...

In the verse that follows, Jesus Christ signifies to mean what death he should die and how that was to bring about His resurrection. It is important to note that the vision did not rest necessarily on Jesus' death but on His resurrection. One would ask how that's relevant. Let me call your attention that Jesus' death did not automatically warrant a resurrection. In the detail, He needed to destroy him that had the power of death (note: not the power over death), that is, the devil (see Hebrews 2:14) and by his power take again the life He laid (John 10:17-18). So in the book of Revelation chapter one verse eighteen Jesus Christ affirms what He wrought concerning those things that transpired when He went down into hell. He had to take the keys (power) of hell and death if He were to destroy death who is the last enemy (1 Cor 15:26) and consequently cause life into being and thus resurrect.

By this victory, He swallowed death forever. It is in the light of this authority that Jesus Christ procured His resurrection.

> *I am He that lives, and was dead; and, behold, I am alive for evermore, Amen; and* **have the keys of hell and of death.**
>
> **Revelation 1:18**

Now that Christ resurrected, what it meant was that the second part of the vision – **"will draw all men unto me"** - was committed into action. In other words we are in that time of scripture where **"all men shall be drawn to Jesus Christ"** (emphasis on "all men"). So that the timing and plan of God to fulfill His agenda by this mystery of the Feast of Weeks as we saw earlier is perfectly and nicely carried out by the hand of the Almighty God. It is in these acts of God that our trust in Him and the truth we all seek is corroborated. It is like a man who finds a treasure hid in a field, and sells all he has to buy that field (Matthew 13:44).

It is not surprising that the devil did and continues to deceive the unbelieving world on the truth concerning Christ's resurrection after a failed attempt to hold Him bound in the grave. In times past, everyone who had posed a threat to the devil was eliminated by death like he did with Adam followed by righteous Abraham, Moses, Job and the list continues. And so, when Jesus Christ came on the scene and posed a much bigger threat to the kingdom of hell, the devil worked through Judas Iscariot among others to see that Jesus Christ was put to death; scripture clearly puts it this way "...the devil having now put into the heart of Judas Iscariot, Simon's son to betray Him..." (John 13:2). To the extent that even when Jesus deserved nothing worthy of death after considering the evidence by Pontius Pilate, they forced the hands of the law to seize Him (Luke 23:13-15,23).

The Contention Of His Resurrection

> *Except it be for this one voice, that I cried standing among them, touching THE RESURRECTION OF THE DEAD I AM CALLED IN QUESTION BY YOU THIS DAY.*
>
> *Acts 24:21*

The subject of Jesus Christ's resurrection and in a broader sense the resurrection of the dead has been keenly contested among sects and other religious bodies both in the past and in the present. Others who somewhat identify with Him in some way have purported His resurrection to mean He substituted for another to take His place – which we know is false in the face of concrete evidence. To this extent, sects of higher power able to influence a following have concocted stories to vilify the truth that Jesus Christ – the Saviour of the world – rose from the grave (see also Acts 25: 18-19). In St. Matthew's gospel reading from the twenty-eighth chapter we see it clearer how these sects did everything to conceal the truth even in those early days of His resurrection.

[11]Now when they were going, behold, some of the watch came into the city, and shewed unto the chief priests all the things that were done.

[12] And when they were assembled with the elders, and had taken counsel, they gave large money unto the soldiers,

[13] SAYING, SAY YE, HIS DISCIPLES CAME BY NIGHT, AND STOLE HIM AWAY WHILE WE SLEPT.

[14] And if this come to the governor's ears, we will persuade him, and secure you.

15 SO THEY TOOK THE MONEY, AND DID AS THEY WERE TAUGHT: AND THIS SAYING IS COMMONLY REPORTED AMONG THE JEWS UNTIL THIS DAY.

Matthew 28:11-15

It is very much incredible that soldiers, most likely of the best and of very high ranking due to the nature of the task (Command therefore that the sepulchre be made sure until the third day, lest his disciples come by night, and steal him away, and say unto the people, **He is risen from the dead**: so the last error shall be worse than the first.- Matt 27:64) – to secure the very thing they were warned against decides to accept money to keep their mouth shut on the truth. Obviously, you can tell the plot in the effort of those who wanted to conceal the truth by all means. It is no surprise that some many years after the death and resurrection of Jesus Christ, by many infallible proofs, people still contest the subject of Jesus Christ's resurrection. It is worth mentioning again that it was the subject of contention when the Apostle Paul was brought before Felix, Festus and King Agrippa (see Acts 25, 26, 27).

The question then comes to mind: why would those who witnessed and knew the truth about Jesus Christ's resurrection would want to lie about it? Was it just about the resurrection? Does it all end with the resurrection? I dare say, it's just the beginning.

In Paul's first epistle to the Corinth he tells us:

> *⁷ But we speak **the wisdom of God in a mystery, even the hidden wisdom**, which God ordained before the world unto our glory:*

> *⁸ Which none of the princes of this world knew: for had they known it, **they would not have crucified the Lord of glory.**__*

> ***1 Corinthians 2:7-8***

"...crucified the Lord of glory".

I am sure that should ring a bell by now – His crucifixion!

Jesus Christ's death and resurrection is sequel to the glory ordained. That is, it is what validates His vision – what He sets to accomplish so as to roll out the force of His mission – how to get this done. It is in this that we access what it takes to get it all done – 'ALL-POWER' which works by the mystery of tongues speaking! Otherwise, the mystery could not be substantiated. In a much simpler way, Jesus Christ's death released 'ALL-POWER' from the hands of the devil (remember he stole it from Adam) and the mystery of tongues accesses that realm of 'ALL-POWER' for delivery of the ingathering agenda.

> *[12] Now if Christ be preached that he rose from the dead, how say some among you that there is no resurrection of the dead?*
>
> *1 Corinthians 15:12*

The Mission Statement:

It is no coincidence that after Jesus Christ demonstrated His vision of being lifted from the earth, He makes this ever profound statement:

> *And Jesus came and spake unto them, saying, ALL POWER IS GIVEN UNTO ME IN HEAVEN AND IN EARTH.GO YE THEREFORE,*
>
> *Matthew 28:18-19 (paraphrased)*

In this verse of scripture, Jesus Christ states His mission – ALL POWER IS GIVEN TO ME, THEREFORE GO. Connecting both the vision and mission statement would mean **"TO DRAW ALL MEN UNTO ME IS**

BY ALL POWER AND THIS IS GIVEN TO ME, THEREFORE GO!"

The mission, that is, "the how" is clearly spelt out. Jesus Christ is saying we will need 'all-power' to draw all men in delivery of the ingathering of the harvest.

Chapter
four

All-Power

Power is in levels and when you check through scripture, you will also discover that power is in dispensations. What do I mean? By God's own design, a corresponding power is required to deliver a corresponding effect per time. It is in light of this that we need to understand the power dimension made available in these last days for the delivery of the ingathering of the harvest! Don't forget as we have mentioned earlier, the principal purpose of Jesus' death and resurrection (vision and mission statement) was to reclaim the all-power the devil stole from Adam through deception and by same draw all men to Himself – man's original estate!

Let's consider some clear examples on the subject of 'all-power' in scripture.

The seventy

When Jesus Christ sent out the seventy in Luke's gospel chapter ten verse one through to nineteen, emphasis on verse nineteen, He gave them power. Consequently, this power could only take them as far as certain parts of Israel. But in Matthew's gospel chapter twenty-eight verses eighteen, when He had descended and ascended from hell, said He unto His disciples: "All power is given unto me, therefore go! Go into all the nations, teach them... "All nations"! Yes, "all nations"!! Every part on the globe including strong Islamic, Communist nations among others. The reason most believers are yet to fully actualize this truth is because of a lack of 'all-power'. Yes we have some power, no doubt, but to invade all nations we must engage what Jesus Christ describes as 'all-power'.

The Devil's Testimony

Another scripture that validates the eternal truth of 'all-power' is found in Luke's gospel chapter four verse six:

> *And the devil said unto him,* **All** *this* **power** *will I give thee, and* **the glory** *of them:* **for that is delivered unto me; and to whomsoever I will I give it.**

In the mouth of two every word shall be established. That is, this scripture confirms the subject of 'all-power' and eliminates every attempt of the devil to blur the vision of the saints to think of this truth as a mere play of words. "ALL THIS POWER" - this was the devil speaking to deliver unto Jesus Christ the 'all-power' he stole from Adam if Jesus Christ would bow to him. Indeed, even the devil acknowledges the subject of all-power!! Then as Christians, we need a full grasp of this subject. If it wasn't important for our ministry as ordained by Jesus Christ, He wouldn't have taken it out of the devil's hand before commanding go! In detail, this is the 'all-power' God gave Adam when he introduced man into the God-head (this is how much sin cost God and how much He loved us to have made us a part of the Godhead).

Jesus' Instruction In His Absence

And he said unto them, when I sent you without purse, and scrip, and shoes, lacked ye anything? And they said, nothing.

*Then said he unto them, **but now, he that hath a purse, let him take it, and likewise his scrip: and he that hath no sword, let him sell his garment, and buy one.***

Luke 22:35-36

Interesting! When Jesus Christ was with the disciples, they needed neither purse, scrip nor shoes, and the disciples confirmed that (Luke 9). Why? We see the answer emphatic in Luke's gospel chapter nine verse one through to three

Then he called his twelve disciples together, and gave them power and authority *over all devils, and to cure diseases*

And he sent them to preach the kingdom of God, and to heal the sick.

And he said unto them, Take nothing for your journey, neither staves, nor scrip, neither

> *bread, neither money; neither have two coats*
> *apiece.*

"...He gave them"! Who gave them? Jesus Christ gave them, the disciples, power and authority! But you may ask, what has power and authority got to do with purse, scrip and shoes? Good question. And the answer is, it has everything to do with anything that is named or created. Power and for that matter, authority is what upholds the whole of creation (upholding all things by the word of His POWER – Hebrews 1:3). In other words, power is the source of all that we see! With power, you have everything responding to you! All things are at your beck and call!!! No wonder the disciples lacked nothing when Jesus sent them out because they possessed in their hands what it takes to get all – POWER. Friends, can I tell you this; the reason you've lacked so far or seem to feel inadequate at the LORD's commission to go is because you lack that one and vital thing required to get all – POWER. When you attain that status by positioning yourself, you get it all, nothing lacking. Absolutely nothing!!

However, why would Jesus Christ now command that they got those things which once were not required –

purse, scrip and sword (Luke 22:36)? Why would the Master now say a thing as this? I can imagine the look of surprise on the face of the disciples. 'What do you mean, Jesus?', I suppose, were the thoughts that ran through their minds for the shock that was thrown at them. 'We trusted you Jesus', was probably what Thomas thought. Again, why now? And this was what Jesus had to say:

> ***...for the things concerning me have an end.***
> ***Luke 22:37c***

In detail, Jesus Christ meant – I gave you power when I sent you out (Luke 9:1-3) but I go away. While I was with you, I did what the Father commanded me. In the meantime, I must contend for your own power which the Father gave man at creation but Adam lost to the devil. I go away with mine, Jesus meant, but I shall bring you yours, so for this short time you are on your own. Remember, Jesus Christ never lost His power to the devil. In fact, satan acknowledged it when the demons (his agents) said "Jesus I know" (Acts 19:15). If Jesus ever lost His power, then He was in no place to defeat the devil. So what Jesus contended for when He descended into hell was not His personal power rather that of man! Thus, it was time for man to be restored like it was in the beginning in the garden by the work of Jesus Christ. Jesus Christ was bringing man into the realm of 'ALL-POWER' – take note as according to Matthew 28:18. In other words, Jesus was telling Peter and the rest of the disciples and everyone who should believe their gospel that He was upgrading them from the realm of power and authority (what Jesus Christ gave them while He was with them in the flesh) to ALL-POWER (the personal power they shall receive after His resurrection) to do the work of the ingathering of the harvest. Therefore, Jesus Christ by this was ushering us into a new realm but until then they will be naked of the power He (Jesus Christ) once gave them when He was with them. Also by this, Jesus Christ closed the previous chapter and opened a new one – 'ALL-POWER'. This was Jesus' concluding remarks concerning the disciples being clothed with power:

"...It is not for you to know the times or seasons which the Father has put in His own power. But you shall receive power after that the Holy Ghost is come upon you and you shall be witnesses unto me both in Jerusalem and in all Judea and in Samaria and unto the outermost part of the earth"! (Acts 1:7-8). Brethren we are in those days of 'ALL-POWER' – it's official.

A sequel to this is Peter's betrayal of Jesus Christ. Peter did not betray his Master because he wanted to. In fact, it was the last thing that he could imagine himself do judging from his own words:

> *And he said unto him,* **Lord, I am ready to go with thee, both into prison, and to death.**
>
> **Luke 22:33**

Peter meant every word he spoke to Jesus Christ. However, words were not enough to sustain his intent. Peter needed more than that. To uphold what he spoke, he needed power – the word of His power (Heb 1:3). Meanwhile, that power which he once had and by it worked hitherto was suspended. Peter could not discern to understand what Jesus Christ meant in Luke 22:31-37. That was Peter's downfall and this could have been very detrimental. It was possible he could have never survived that guilt of betraying his dearly beloved Master Jesus Christ. We may not have heard of Peter again as like Judas Iscariot and all the great things the LORD worked through him. His faith would have failed completely but thanks be to God who through Jesus' prayer and mercies restored him.

And the Lord said, Simon, Simon, behold, Satan hath desired to have you, that he may sift you as wheat:

***But I have prayed for thee, THAT THY FAITH FAIL NOT:** and when thou art converted, strengthen thy brethren.*

Luke 22:31-32

Friends, it is important to understand the times and power stage available for the full functionality lest your faith fails. But your faith shall not fail in the name of Jesus Christ.

Paul's Revelation – "The Power Of His Resurrection"

The Apostle Paul identifies himself as the least of the Apostles to mean that he was probably the last to have joined in this apostleship after the death and resurrection of Jesus Christ. Otherwise, he did not have the opportunity to walk with Jesus in the days of his flesh as the others. That also meant, he was not present when the subject of 'ALL-POWER' was introduced by Jesus Christ according to Matthew's gospel chapter twenty-eight verse eighteen and nineteen. He didn't get a firsthand knowledge on the subject like Peter and the rest. However, in the course of his ministry when the subject of all-power was revealed unto him, he desired to know it and walked in the fullness of it.

> ***For I neither received it of man, neither was I taught it, but by the revelation of Jesus Christ.***
>
> ***Gal 1:12***

Now let's look at Paul's revelation on the subject.

According to Philippians 3:10, Paul tells the Church about his newly found revelation of what was once, first mentioned by Jesus Christ to the disciples after he had resurrected from the grave:

> *That I may know him, and* **THE POWER OF HIS RESURRECTION,** *and the fellowship of his sufferings,* **being made conformable unto his death;**

...The Power of His Resurrection! ...being made conformable unto His Death!!

Do these ring a bell? The subject of ALL-POWER was never mentioned by Jesus Christ until after His resurrection. All the while, Jesus gave them power.

Please note there is a big difference between POWER and ALL-POWER. This is not just trying to play with words but a spiritual and eternal truth that must be received. The Apostle Paul understood this revelation clearly when he received it. No wonder he walked in this realm so much that the devils acknowledged him after Jesus Christ:

> ***And the evil spirit answered and said, Jesus I know, and Paul I know;...***
>
> *Acts 9:15*

ALL-POWER is what the Apostle Paul refers to as the **THE POWER OF HIS RESURRECTION** – the power Jesus rose with from the grave which he delivered since the day of Pentecost for the ingathering of the harvest! This 'all-power" is available for these last days and accessible on the platform of tongues speaking. The Church must understand and walk in the consciousness of this essential arsenal for the delivery of the times.

Chapter

five

Pray Ye the Lord of The Harvest

Now, if there was ever a battle to fight, then I must say it is the battle to see the Church of God built. It is in relation to this that Jesus Christ the Author of the Church says I will build my Church and the gates of hell shall not prevail against it (Matthew 16:18). This is clear indication of a battle. Meaning, though prophecy is gone ahead and the plan for execution properly placed, there's still the need to war them into fulfillment. In spite of this, in many instances, we have seen the majority engage in every battle but the battle to build the Church of God. We have fought the battle against any devil that dared our homes, marriage, fruitfulness of the womb, health, and finance among others with every pint of blood in us and have seen the battles go in our favour – in fact we go great lengths, out of the usual to ensure those victories. I have witnessed quite a few prayer sessions where the momentum of prayer rose when such prayer subjects were matters that concerned our personal wellbeing and momentum dropped when such prayers as it were, were not directly connected to us. Please don't get me wrong, I am not saying that praying personal supplication is wrong; I am only pointing out the need for the right application in both instances. The foundation of any proper building must be laid first then the bricks and not the other way.

The Church is that foundation and when the Church is well positioned then the remaining will fall in line. In Matthew's gospel chapter six verse thirty three, Jesus Christ strengthens this truth to say - seek the Kingdom of God first and every other thing meaning every other thing shall be added onto you. Now this is the real battle that should preoccupy us every single moment. If you are a redeemed child of God having escaped the kingdom of darkness because the battle for your soul was taken up by another redeemed child who probably never knew you or met you but prayed day and night, in fasting and prayers to see that hold of the devil on your soul lost so you can be freed into the marvelous light of Jesus Christ, then it is only reasonable to do same for another soul. My Bishop, Bishop David O. Oyedepo, once said "people don't just get saved, it is the result of your prayers and reaching out to them". A classic example from scripture is a man with like passion as most of us – not an ordained Apostle or Bishop or Prophet to say that he did what he did because he was separated to such an office but just a servant of the LORD – the man Epaphras who laboured passionately in prayers for the saints that they may stand perfect.

> *Epaphras, who is one of you, a servant of Christ, saluteth you,* **always labouring fervently for you in prayers, that ye may stand perfect and complete in all the will of God.**
>
> **Colossians 4:12**

Above all is the example of Jesus Christ when He prayed for those that believed on Him and those that would believe afterwards in John's gospel chapter seventeen verses nine following:

⁹ I pray for them: I pray not for the world, but for them which thou hast given me; for they are thine.

¹¹ And now I am no more in the world, but these are in the world, and I come to thee. **Holy Father, keep through thine own name those whom thou hast given me, that they may be one, as we are.**

*¹² **While I was with them in the world, I kept them in thy name: those that thou gavest me I have kept, and none of them is lost,** but the son of perdition; that the scripture might be fulfilled.*

¹⁵ I pray not that thou shouldest take them out of the world, but that thou shouldest keep them from the evil.

²⁰ Neither pray I for these alone, but for them also which shall believe on me through their word;

²¹ That they all may be one; as thou, Father, art in me, and I in thee, that they also may be one in us: that the world may believe that thou hast sent me.

John 17: 9,11,12,15,20,21

Who Are We Up Against?

The first step to winning any battle is to know who you're up against. This is crucial because a wrong judgment of who the real enemy is means a blatant failure. There is the story of a soldier who fought wars for wages. So, the king of one kingdom contracted him to fight the other kingdoms because they were enemies of his kingdom who wanted to destroy his kingdom. Little did this soldier know that the real enemy was this king who contracted him. He wanted to enslave the other kingdoms so he could be lord over them. In the end, this soldier defeated the other kingdoms making this king so powerful and ended up being captured by the same king he fought for.

Irrespective of who committed the act of sin or did evil, it is important to acknowledge the root of the evil. It is only in this way we know that by dealing with the root there shall be no insurgence of such evil. The problem is not with the act as it were, it is of the root. There again, one must be held accountable for their actions/choice but we should not be oblivious of the root cause. In the example of the mad man at the tomb of Gadara, we understand that the root of his problem was those unclean spirits that possessed him. This made him very violent and did things that one in a good state of mind would not do. But after he met Jesus Christ and He cast out those unclean spirits, for they were many, scripture accounts that this man came to his right senses.

> *And they came to Jesus, and seeing him that was possessed with the devil, and had the legion, sitting, and clothed, and in his right mind: and they were afraid.*
>
> *Mark 5:15*

Another very striking instance is that of the High Priest Joshua in the book of Zechariah chapter three reading from verse one through to five where satan went out purposely to resist the chosen priest of God to defile him. Can I say this, this is true wickedness. Things don't just happen – they are controlled or influenced to happen from the spirit realm. It is in light of this that we know for sure who we are in battle against.

> *And he shewed me Joshua the high priest standing before the angel of the Lord, and Satan standing at his right hand to resist him.*

And the Lord said unto Satan, The Lord rebuke thee, O Satan; even the Lord that hath chosen Jerusalem rebuke thee: is not this a brand plucked out of the fire?

Now Joshua was clothed with filthy garments, and stood before the angel.

And he answered and spake unto those that stood before him, saying, **Take away the filthy garments from him. And unto him he said, Behold, I have caused thine iniquity to pass from thee, and I will clothe thee with change of raiment.**

And I said, Let them set a fair mitre upon his head. So they set a fair mitre upon his head, and clothed him with garments. And the angel of the Lord stood by.

Zechariah 3:1-5

In this last example is the cause of all the world's problems you can think of; from wars to famine, diseases, crime, violence, murders, hatred, drug addiction, lust and the list never ends. It is the root cause for the eternal condemnation of any man who will not accept the redemptive work of Jesus Christ.

I mean eternal destruction, one without end – just imagine. Think of the people who ignorantly have staunch positions in what they believe is truth only to find out, if they ever allow themselves, that they had believed a well-crafted lie from the pit of hell – just imagine. This is the example of the fall of the first man and woman; Adam and Eve. It is the sole reason for the scripture – "For all have sinned and come short of the glory of God" and "so death passed upon all men, for that all have sinned" (Romans 3:23, 5:12). I have asked myself severally why the devil would not leave Adam and Eve to be but went into that garden to make them do that one thing, the only thing God had commanded Adam and Eve not to because He (God) knew the gravity of its consequence as we see in God's own statement to the woman – *what is this that thou has done?"* (Genesis 3:13). Why? Why this wickedness from the devil? But scripture makes us understand that the devil is the author of sin (I John 3:8) – all he does is to plan and devise evil. There is no good in him at all (John 8:44). I want you to know the root cause of the problems we have in the world today. I want you to see who is to be held responsible for all the evil and in the event one does not accept the redemptive work of Jesus Christ, will suffer that fate of eternal condemnation in hell and the lake of fire – this is no fiction or fables (II Peter 1:16a). I want you to know it, see it, in every circumstance seemingly and as a result develop a strong godly hatred that will propel you into battle against this wickedness. To stand and fight because it is your personal business. To pray it until it be all said and done! Because if our gospel be hid, it is hid to them that are lost: in whom the god of this world who is the devil hath blinded the minds of them which believe not, lest the light of the glorious gospel of Christ, who is the image of God, should shine unto them (II Corinthians 4:3-4 paraphrased). Can I say this to you, now this is the real battle and we are up against the devil. Somehow the devil has deceived some to thinking that God is to blame for that plane crash, that hereditary disease, that defect from birth, the death of your beloved one among others. As a result, some have lost sight of the real enemy who is the devil. Let me say this emphatically – everything that God did was very good and by extension God can only do good (Gen 1:31).

In Paul's epistle to the Ephesians in chapter six verses twelve; Paul exposes the believer positioned for battle to the real enemy, the devil and his agents:

> *For we wrestle not against flesh and blood, but against principalities, against powers, against the rulers of the darkness of this world, against spiritual wickedness in high places.*

Ephesians 6:12

The battle for the souls of men is primarily spiritual and the reason for which our engagement must be essentially spiritual. Israel's four hundred and thirty years of bondage in Egypt was not because Pharaoh held them down, but the gods of Egypt did the worse. And until God brought judgment upon the gods of Egypt, Israel was never freed from bondage – "ye were bondmen"

> *For I will pass through the land of Egypt this night, and will smite all the firstborn in the land of Egypt, both man and beast;* **and against all the gods of Egypt I will execute judgment: I am the Lord.**

Exodus 12:12

In another instance is Nicodemus' assertion of the impossibility of the natural dimension to execute a thing such as this in his question – how can this thing be? (John 3:4). And the great mystery of the process of new birth– that which is born of the Spirit is spirit, Jesus said (John 3:6).

What To Do?

> *Therefore said he unto them, The harvest truly is great, but the labourers are few:* **pray ye therefore the Lord of the harvest,** *that He would send forth labourers into his harvest.*
>
> *Luke 10:2*

Jesus the Christ acknowledged the enormity of the harvest and commands us to do this – "pray ye the Lord of the harvest". In other words, as much as the prophecy has been foretold, we must commit to praying harvest-centered prayers to engage the LORD of the harvest – pray the LORD concerning the harvest. If Jesus Christ affirmed the vastness of the ingathering agenda, then it meant that supernatural help is required – it cannot be accomplished in the strength of the flesh. Who is the Lord of the harvest?

> *Now the Lord is that Spirit: and where the Spirit of the Lord is, there is liberty.*
>
> *2 Corinthians 3:17*

In this scripture we see and understand in plain language that the Holy Spirit is the LORD of the harvest. He is the Chairman of the feast of weeks – the harvest. He is the Mastermind ensuring that things are done and fulfilled according as the Father has planned it. He makes bare the will of God and those strategies to get it executed. And one direct and unhindered channel to the Holy Ghost is the mystery of tongues speaking. Jesus Christ is the baptizer of the Holy Ghost and the Holy Ghost gives the utterances of the tongues(Matt 3:11, Acts 2:4).

I have been faced with instances where I engaged the mystery of speaking in tongues to receive divine direction on major decisions of life, to get instant help from superiors and find missing items among others. I believe you reading this have had similar experiences while engaging the mystery of speaking in unknown tongues. However, most of these if not all have been the secondary application of this mystery. Jesus Christ in Luke's gospel chapter ten and verse two shows us what to do about the harvest – (I suppose by now you understand the harvest from the preceding chapters and how they are all connected to the mystery of the feast of weeks and therefore its connection with the mystery of tongues speaking). He says –"pray ye the Lord of the harvest"! This demonstration of the mystery of tongues speaking is evident in Acts chapter two.

So Now The Question Will Be How Do I Speak Or What Do I Speak?

My assignment here as directed by the Holy Ghost is simple – not to teach on tongues speaking in detail but to connect the mystery of the feast of weeks and the place of tongues speaking to expedite the mission at hand. I believe authors like Kenneth Hagin of blessed memory in his book *"Tongues Beyond The Upper Room"*, Bishop David Oyedepo's *"Conquering Controlling Powers"* among others have done a brilliant job on the subject. Let me quickly add that the author of the book of Romans - the Apostle Paul – an apostle chosen personally by Jesus Christ when He appeared to him on his way to Damascus much more opened the Church up on the subject (Act 26:12-18). It is thus important to consider Paul's understanding of the subject of tongues speaking as taught him by the Holy Ghost (1 Cor 14:18, Gal 1:11-12)

What or how to speak is as seen in verse twenty seven of Romans chapter eight:

^27 And he that searcheth the hearts knoweth what is the mind of the Spirit, because he maketh intercession for the saints according to the will of God.

Romans 8:27

And He That Searcheth The Hearts...

The heart is the seat of the Spirit. He relays every information there. The heart is sometimes referred to as the spirit man. The Holy Spirit doth bear witness with our spirit man (Rom 8:16). What or how to speak (tongues) is in the heart – the spirit, which is the spirit of the believer. Thus a search or attention to your spirit will cause the outflow of the deposits – tongues. And I must say that it is the purest form of the will of God. The result is that all things begin to work for the believer to actualize the mission. It is interesting how *all-power* connects to *all things* working! I once did not believe in the mystery of tongues speaking because of my background. At this time I thought I had a sound theology on the subject which asserted that what people spoke were gibberish. Yes they might have been an abuse of this power for those who thought of it lightly but does not take away the genuine power. You can only have the counterfeit of the original or the counterfeit is the proof that the original exists. Can I tell you this, there are realms of the ingathering agenda you can't access except by the mystery of tongues speaking. It is in those realms your spirit comes into total unity with the Spirit of God to know what and how to speak. And it is what is spoken as commanded by God that finds fulfillment in this Kingdom of our God. A typical example is that of Ezekiel the prophet and the valley of dry bones – "So I prophesied as I was commanded (Ezekiel 37:7)

I was led by the inspiration of the Holy Ghost to understand Romans 8:26-28 as this:

> *Likewise, the Holy Spirit helps our weakness especially in the area of prayer. Of course, as far as prayer is concerned, we miss it! In view of this, the Holy Spirit gives unto us in our spirit man exactly as God would have us pray expecting us to openly pray them.*

> *We can trust what the Holy Spirit relays in our spirit man to pray because it is the exact will of God per time. How do we know this? Only the Holy Spirit knows the mind of God*

By connecting to this realm we access ALL POWER and for certainty ALL THINGS begin to work together producing as God in creation – knowing that whatever God spoke into being He saw that it was good. Thus our love for God proven by our heart for the harvest delivers maximally to fulfil His purpose.

So don't sit unconcerned. Take up the battle in prayer exercising the mystery of tongues speaking, releasing all-power for the ingathering of the harvest. Don't be slack, lift up the hands which hang down, and the feeble knees!

Chapter

six

Walk In The Spirit

If we live in the Spirit, let us also walk in the Spirit.

Gal 5:25

The life of the Spirit is paramount in these last days. You will understand from where we began till now that the Holy Spirit is in charge of this massive ingathering agenda. The last days have been committed to Him. He is that "Wind" still hovering over creation like we saw in Genesis chapter one that consequently brought order to the earth and the "rushing mighty wind Holy Ghost baptism" that gathered the multitudes at Pentecost. Like His name,

He is spirit – we cannot see or relate with Him with the five natural senses. No! We can only relate with Him in the realm of the spirit. To the end, we are in constant unison with the Holy Spirit in carrying out the assignment for the hour. Thus, it becomes imperative to walk in the spirit. This is very vital.

Most people have found it somewhat a difficult thing to pray in tongues as a habit (don't forget the place of tongues in carrying out the ingathering agenda of the last days). This is largely because majority of people are mostly absent in the Spirit. As such, you would observe that in a meeting, usually, you would need to create an atmosphere for the flow. And when that is done, you see praying in tongues takes an increasing dimension. This is a common observation. Thus walking in the Spirit among other things, is simply creating the atmosphere for flowing in and with the Spirit at all time. That is, to go live in the Spirit like going live on TV. In other words, to be responsive to the slightest signal from the Holy Spirit at any time. This is very vital as the LORD of the harvest is always on the go, delivering the will of God per time in fulfilment of the ingathering agenda. Note, God always, at every time has a mind and what he wants fulfilled. And it is these happenings that culminate in the whole. For instance, in the life of the Apostles and those of the early Church, you would see this as a common phenomenon. Concerning Peter it is reported "while Peter thought on the vision, the Spirit said unto him, behold, three men seek thee. Arise therefore, and get thee down, and go with them, doubting nothing: for I have sent them" (Acts 10:19-20). John the Apostle recounted; "I was in the Spirit on the LORD's day and I heard..." (Rev 1:10). In Acts 8:29 we see "then the Spirit said unto Philip, go near, and join thyself to this chariot." All these and many others are manifestations of the Spirit in the lives of men who walked in the Spirit. So you see why it is vital to walk in the Holy Spirit in fulfillment of the ingathering agenda. Again, you would notice that every successful ministry has been the effect of a continuous reliance on the Holy Spirit for His leadings. That is, taking the responsibility to connect with the Holy Spirit on every matter. And this is why:

> *But God hath revealed them unto us by His Spirit: for the Spirit searcheth all things, yea, the deep things of God.*

For what man knoweth the things of a man, save the spirit of man which is in him? even so the things of God knoweth no man, but the Spirit of God.

Now we have received, not the spirit of the world, but the spirit which is of God; that we might know the things that are freely given to us of God.

***Which things also we speak**, not in the words which man's wisdom teacheth, but **which the Holy Ghost teacheth**; comparing spiritual things with spiritual.*

But the natural man receiveth not the things of the Spirit of God: for they are foolishness unto him: neither can he know them, because they are spiritually discerned.

I Cor 2:10-14

There again we see another striking thing;

Which things also we speak, ... in the words ... which the Holy Ghost teacheth

You would notice here that, by walking in the Spirit we gain high-speed access to the things to speak which only the Holy Ghost teaches. This should strike a chord – tongues speaking. Thus by aligning/walking in the Holy Ghost, we bolster the mystery of tongues speaking which is God's arsenal to deliver the harvest. And you can expect all things to begin to work!

Now let me draw your attention to something very important on this subject of walking in the Spirit. The feat of Moses to have brought the people of Israel out of bondage in Egypt could not have been possible if Moses did not hear from God per time in Egypt. In fact Pharaoh would have killed him so easily if he ever missed God's directive. So you would see in several places; "and the LORD said to Moses..." (Now the Lord is that Spirit: and where the Spirit of the Lord is, there is liberty – 2 Cor 3:17). This was Moses' greatest secret. This is a wakeup call for all.

How Do I Know I Am Walking In The Spirit?

Walking in the Spirit is not necessarily putting on a sanctimonious look with a soft and gentle speech. No! The acid test to walking in the Spirit is what is described as the fruit of the Spirit. It is the law that governs walking in the Spirit – against such there is no law! In other words, if the fruit of the Spirit is evident in an ever growing dimension in you; you will not struggle walking in the Spirit.

> *But the fruit of the Spirit is love, joy, peace, longsuffering, gentleness, goodness, faith, meekness, temperance: against such there is no law*
>
> *Gal 5:22-23*

It will be of interest to note that many have struggled with walking or flowing in the Spirit. Majority have thought of it as an impossible task and one reserved for the few in the prophetic calling. Can I tell you this, that's a big lie. As much as you are engaged in this ingathering agenda, it your rightful privilege. Examine yourself daily and keep pressing on walking in the Spirit. For starters, it may seem as not yielding any result but keep at it and before you know it you shall be on the highway. The Holy Spirit is ever ready to welcome you on this journey with Him. For those who have come thus far in this regard, we still have a long way to go. Our ultimate is the Garden of Eden experience where God would come and commune with man.

Chapter
seven

The Trap of the Ingathering of the Harvest

After Israel was harnessed out of the land of bondage, Egypt (Exodus 13:13), they were now come between Egypt and the Promised Land. God had to try the mixed multitude – to gather the harvest of Israel into the Promised Land. This was not the end of their redemption, rather it was just beginning. They had to go through the wilderness, cross the Red sea on dry ground, access food and water in the wilderness, fight and conquer the Amorites, Hittites, Perizzites, Canaanites, Jebusites, and Girgashites that inhabited the land. In fact leaving Egypt was just getting started. Therefore God would not take them through the way of the

Philistines which was near but led them through the way of the Red sea otherwise they would see war and return to Egypt (Exodus 13:17-18). So Israel began their journey to the Promised Land.

One major scene that characterized the transition from the land of bondage to the Promise Land was *murmuring* right from the everyday person to leaders who were given the responsibility to do the service of the tabernacle unto the LORD including Korah and his company who rebelled and provoked God's anger to consume them (Numbers 16:1-40). Amazingly, the day after God had destroyed Korah, Dathan and Abiram and their company, the children of Israel murmured again. And the LORD apart from destroying the company of Korah, fourteen thousand seven hundred people were destroyed that day.

> *But on the morrow all the congregation of **the children of Israel murmured against Moses and against Aaron**, saying, Ye have killed the people of the Lord*
>
> ***....Now they that died in the plague were fourteen thousand and seven hundred, beside them that died about the matter of Korah.***
>
> *Numbers 16:41,49*

In another place and much more, this same episode of murmuring cost Moses and Aaron their place in the Promised Land. God had said to Moses to speak to the Rock: that water would flow for the children of Israel. In the midst of unbearable murmurings from the children of Israel, Moses and Aaron disobeyed God and struck the Rock twice (Numbers 20:12). This is just but one of the many devastating effects of murmuring Israel suffered. I have wondered why these murmurings never ceased, judging from previous experiences of God's great salvation. Couldn't they have asked God rather than murmur to keep provoking Him to wrath? Consequently, no one of that generation entered the Promised Land except Caleb and Joshua.

How Sensitive Is The Subject Of Murmuring?

To murmur against God is to mean that "God you can't do anything or what you claim – it's just empty noise!" In essence, it is to mock the integrity of God – I mean God's integrity. No one dares that! Now that is what murmuring is. Anytime you murmur against God you are mocking His integrity as God! Even in the earthly, you don't just touch people's hard earned integrity, they will hit back at you especially in the case it is not what is purported. Our God is a jealous God, you don't touch His integrity; He will finish you! So watch it.

> *And the Lord spake unto Moses and Aaron,* **Because ye believed me not, to sanctify me in the eyes of the children of Israel,** *therefore ye shall not bring this congregation into the land which I have given them.*
>
> ***Numbers 20:12***

At the water of Meribah where Moses and Aaron disobeyed God because they did not heed to the instruction from God, God said because you did not sanctify me before the people – you did not show my integrity before the people, therefore you will not cross to the Promise Land. You shall fall here like the others and on mount Hor, Aaron died and Moses followed thereafter. You don't touch the integrity of God, you don't!! God said, "Moses, because you did not sanctify me before the people, therefore you and Aaron shall not cross to the Promised Land! Perhaps, you would ask, "God, but Moses had obeyed you all the while, why this?" "Moreover, he *just* struck the Rock twice – yes, You mentioned he should just speak to the Rock but he struck it out of anger. It wasn't his fault;

the people pushed him to. LORD, why?" The answer is simple - because, Moses touched the integrity of God. And even Moses of all prophets of whom it is testified saying there had not risen any such as Moses who saw God in a similitude (Deuteronomy 34:10), God did not spare him! Let's watch it!! That is what murmuring does. You mock the integrity of God, you pay dearly for it!

> *For the Lord shall rise up as in mount Perazim, he shall be wroth as in the valley of Gibeon, that he may do his work, his strange work; and bring to pass his act, his strange act.*
>
> ***Now therefore be ye not mockers, lest your bands be made strong: for I have heard from the Lord God of hosts a consumption, even determined upon the whole earth.***
>
> *Isaiah 28:21-22*

Israel, to say the older generation, lost the promise of the land that flowed with milk and honey because of the blindfold weapon of murmuring. They missed the ultimate experience of their salvation. Israel could have used a few days for the transit but for their murmurings they suffered wasted years in the wilderness.

And the Lord spoke unto Moses and unto Aaron, saying,

How long shall I bear with this evil congregation, which murmur against me? I have heard the murmurings of the children of Israel, which they murmur against me.

Your carcasses shall fall in this wilderness; and all that were numbered of you, according to your whole number, from twenty years old and upward which have murmured against me.

But as for you, your carcasses, they shall fall in this wilderness.

And your children shall wander in the wilderness forty years, and bear your whoredoms, until your carcasses be wasted in the wilderness

Numbers 14:26-27,29,33

How Does This Apply To The Church?

We are in the era of the great ingathering of the harvest of the souls of men into the storehouse – the mountain of the LORD. 'For other sheep have I', Jesus said, 'which I must bring into the sheepfold' (John 10:16). It is the reason we must guard carefully against the trap of the ingathering. The scriptures are for our learning to understand the times and seasons – so as to respond to the hour of our visitation (Luke 12:44). Let us not be unaware of this seemingly harmless weapon of murmuring deployed by the devil to distract our focus from the season.

The Church of Jesus Christ is God's end time ark of redemption similar to what Israel is in the old covenant. The church is that spiritual Israel. Like Israel was redeemed out of Egypt, so the entire human race is offered redemption from sin through the death and resurrection of our LORD Jesus Christ. Now, it is important to understand according to Solomon that there is nothing new under the sun. It is important we learn from history to guard against any potential mistake. What is the point? If you would watch closely, we are in that period of the great gathering of the harvest. Therefore we will need to look out for the trap of the ingathering of the harvest as the Church is gaining indispensable attention at the world stage, and becoming a major force in these last days in every sector of human endeavour. The Church is becoming more and more aware of her place. She is taking up responsibility, with a supernatural display of great feats and accomplishments the kind we haven't seen done by the Church, great deliverance, great among others ministries. This is to see to our ultimate salvation into the Promised Land of rest, the Sabbath of rest (as we looked at in Chapter one), against which the weapon of murmurings have been deployed. Remember we have said that to murmur is to mock the integrity of God and that has grave consequences in breaching the promise *(Numbers 14:34).*

Now this weapon of murmuring has been deployed on two fronts – internally and externally. Internally, by so called members of the body of Christ castigating ministries doing better and advancing the Kingdom of God here on earth. In their bid, unknowing to them as Korah and his company, are caught in the trap of murmuring as witnessed when Israel journeyed to the Promised Land. Are all the various parts of the body of Christ a hundred percent in line with what God would have us do per time, t? Definitely not! But the good news also is that, there are many ministries (members of the body of Christ) in this present generation who are striving all the time at doing what God would have them do! You are not God their caller, that is to say they don't answer to you! The point is clear – by taking this path, you make yourself vulnerable to the same trap of murmuring that hindered Israel (Numbers 16-1-40). I have asked countless times, after all the miracles, signs and wonders God performed right before the children of Israel anytime they needed it, why would they suddenly forget them all and resort to murmuring the next time they found themselves wanting one thing or the other? Couldn't there be a better way of approaching it? Couldn't they have simply asked God in prayer learning that anytime they murmured, Moses would rather turn to the LORD in prayer and the need was miraculously met? Even after living with Moses for that long, assuming they didn't know the God of their fathers Abraham, Isaac and Jacob, couldn't they have learnt with time, spending that long in the wilderness? Couldn't there had been a better approach rather than murmur? What am I driving at? It will amaze you to know that those who have resorted to murmuring have not for once prayed earnestly concerning the situation for which they murmur, seeking the best way God would have them help in dealing with the situation. It will interest you to know that those who have resorted to murmuring have personal issues they haven't addressed, yet have the effrontery to murmur about others/ministries who have but a little issue and continue to strive for the best. This is caution to all within the body of Christ. If there is something I have learnt on this journey as the LORD taught me is "to mind my own business because that is what I will be accountable for! I am not God!!" Caution there!!

> *Neither murmur ye, as some of them also murmured, and were destroyed of the destroyer.*

> *Now all these things happened unto them for examples: and they are written for our admonition, upon whom the ends of the world are come.*

> *Wherefore let him that thinketh he standeth take heed lest he fall.*
>
> *I Corinthians 10:10-12*

Now, externally, the Church of Christ is also attacked by the same weapon of murmuring. In the book of Numbers chapter twenty two through to twenty three, when Balak, King of Moab, heard of the exploits of Israel redeemed out of Egypt – a type of the Church, he quickly employed the services of Balaam, that he would curse the children of Israel promising to reward him greatly (Numbers 22:17). Balaam would eventually go to meet Balak. But something interesting happens – when Balaam would curse Israel, God will put in his mouth to speak blessings upon Israel.

> *How shall I curse whom God hath not cursed? or how shall I defy, whom the Lord hath not defied?*
>
> *Behold, I have received commandment to bless: and He hath blessed; and I cannot reverse it.*
>
> *Surely there is no enchantment against Jacob, neither is there any divination against Israel: according to this time it shall be said of Jacob and of Israel, What hath God wrought!*
>
> *Numbers 23:8,20,23*

Like it was in the days of Israel when they journeyed into their rest in the Promised Land, so it is with the

Church of Jesus Christ in these last days as the Lord of the harvest gathers the redeemed out of every tongue, kindred, and race. The Church has seen, with the advent of technology and the wide usage of social media, increasing attack by the weapon of murmuring deployed externally. Misrepresentation by perpetuators who desire to carry out their evil deeds have taken the fore. Any matter implicating the Church, even when not thoroughly investigated, is quickly concluded and widespread. The Apostle Paul puts it this way -***For there are many unruly and vain talkers and deceivers... (Titus 1:10).*** Yet when many good things are done by the Church, they are not swift to carry them the same way far and near. Is it coincidental? I dare say no! It is a weapon of murmuring deployed against the Church to distract her from the Promised Land like unto Moses and Aaron. For instance, in recent times there has been heated argument on the covenant of tithing. Countless opinions from diverse groups of people have been expressed, many of whom have no connection with the subject matter whatsoever. These would castigate the Church saying they make enterprise of it and that it should be abolished, taxed, used to cater for the needy and poor in society among others. Of course, to cater for the poor and needy in society is a primary responsibility of the Church, who has not neglected that, but also the duty of every human being. And I can say for a fact, there are ministries that have budget allocation for the poor and needy in society, contributing towards human needs in diverse areas including potable water, schools, scholarships, trainings among many others. Ministries with prudent financial spending, budget allocation, proper book keeping of national/international standards. Yet these would not be spoken of. You know why? It is a weapon deployed against the Church like Israel who did not know that Balaam had been hired to curse them because Balak, King of Moab heard of their exploits and imagined to bring them down. Can I tell you this, we have good news! We are not ignorant of the schemes and devices of the devil (2 Corinthians 2:11). Our defence is in the God who has called us – He will fight for us and we shall continue to hold our peace in the mighty name of Jesus Christ, Amen! All we need do is to guard against this attack knowing how to respond as the LORD leads us that we are not distracted and made to fall in the wilderness (that shall not be our portion in the mighty name of Jesus Christ!). Like Joshua we shall say "there failed nothing of any good thing which the Lord had spoken unto the Church of our LORD Jesus Christ; all came to pass – Amen! (Joshua 21:45)

We are in the golden age of the Church, hallelujah! A clear message to the Church is to keep our focus so we are not distracted as long as we continue to do as commanded by God!

Epilogue

I have tried to prove the central theme of this book. I needed to be sure that this was God's idea and not mine. I wanted to be convinced enough that this was going to deliver as God would have it. Because I couldn't just imagine, especially at the early stages of this book, how the mystery of tongues speaking was vital to delivering such great results as far as the Last days are concerned. Added to this is the fact that tongues speaking was not a well understood subject in the Body of Christ both in knowing which is real and understanding what was spoken. This made me to prove it even the more. During one of the days in putting together this material, I asked God another question – "heavy financial resources are required to take the gospel to every tongue and race and kindred (Zec 1:17); so how would the mystery of tongues speaking take care of that? And to my amazement I had this revealing response: "you would recall that the mystery of tongues speaking accesses the power that worked at creation – "all-power". It gives the believer the access to that all-power God demonstrated at creation. This power makes all things work together (Rom 8:28) producing as God in creation including the heavy financial resources; knowing that whatever God spoke into being He saw. This further corroborated the central theme of this material. Therefore with certainty, God has given us this mystery for such a time as this; that by this mystery He would deliver and fulfil His purpose of the ingathering of the harvest according to the prophecy spoken.

ALTAR CALL

LORD Jesus Christ, I accept I am a sinner and I cannot save myself. I belive you died for me and on the third day you rose again for my justification. So that I can be gathered into the house of God. Now I believe I am born again. I am a child of God. Thank You for saving me.

Amen.

If you prayed this prayer by faith in Jesus Christ, congratulations. You are now a child of God. We would like to connect with you and be helpers of your joy. Send us your name, and contact via tfow.newbirth@gmail. com.